Liberty, Equality, and Revolution
in Alexis de Tocqueville

Liberty, Equality, and Revolution in Alexis de Tocqueville

Irving M. Zeitlin Washington University

LITTLE, BROWN AND COMPANY   BOSTON

FIRST PRINTING

Published simultaneously in Canada
by Little, Brown & Company (Canada) Limited

PRINTED IN THE UNITED STATES OF AMERICA

For my father and in memory of my mother

Preface

THIS STUDY is a short critical introduction to the main social and political ideas of Alexis de Tocqueville, the distinguished nineteenth-century social analyst and observer. Tocqueville never presented his ideas in a very systematic manner, nor does his work lend itself easily to systematic presentation. Therefore, to provide both an exposition and a critical analysis of his ideas, I have designed this study as an *explication de texte,* an extended commentary on his major works. My purpose is to present the main propositions of his social and political thought by examining their relative validity as well as the moral values that apparently underlie them.

To achieve this purpose and to facilitate the exposition, I have compared and contrasted Tocqueville's observations, ideas, and values with those of Karl Marx. (I have devoted one whole section to such a comparison.) As numerous scholars have remarked, the views of these two thinkers in particular virtually beg for comparison. Marx is a natural foil to bring out clearly Tocqueville's views on man, society, history, and politics. Like Marx, and at the same time, Tocqueville recognized the developing historical confrontation between the bourgeoisie and proletariat. Examining their writings, particularly on the revolutions of 1848, therefore affords an excellent opportunity to explore their respective responses, each from a different moral vantage point, to the revolutionary events of the time. The sources of social conflict in Tocqueville's time were not wholly unlike those of our own. An exploration of the similarities and differences between Tocqueville and Marx therefore may help us clarify for the present the various implications of their respective social and political positions.

In general, then, I hope in this study to suggest where Tocqueville erred, and where his insights were valid; where his work is mainly of historical interest, and where it remains relevant to the issues of freedom, equality, and social change.

Contents

Liberty, Equality, and Revolution
in Alexis de Tocqueville

Introduction

ALEXIS DE TOCQUEVILLE retained throughout his life certain aristocratic values he acquired during his childhood. It was not without considerable ambivalence, however, that he did so. Born to a French noble family on July 29, 1805, he lived and wrote at a time when two revolutionary currents, the democratic and the industrial, were markedly transforming the traditional social order of Europe. Tocqueville was concerned with both revolutions (although he understood the former better than the latter, as we shall see), and his interests reveal an unmistakable tension between traditional and modern values — a tension that characterized his writings, his political career, his entire life work.[1] Although he early became convinced of the inevitable advance of democracy and thought efforts to block it quixotic, he nevertheless feared and detested the *demos* socially, culturally, and politically. He feared what he believed was its impending dominion and the consequent erosion, if not outright destruction, of the traditional aristocratic values and institutions. An aristocrat by birth and upbringing, he confronted the intense social conflicts of post-aristocratic nineteenth-century France.

During the French Revolution, Hervé de Tocqueville, his father, a Norman aristocrat, and his mother, also of noble birth, barely escaped the guillotine and spent ten months in prison. After the revolution and

---

[1] For some interesting observations on this tension in Tocqueville's work, see Robert A. Nisbet's article on Tocqueville in the *International Encyclopedia of the Social Sciences*, vol. XVI (New York: Macmillan and Free Press, 1968). And for a discussion of the impact of the democratic and industrial revolutions on the development of sociology in general, including Tocqueville's social thought, see Nisbet's *The Sociological Tradition* (New York: Basic Books, 1966).

the fall of Napoleon, Hervé de Tocqueville fully identified with the restored Bourbons, under whose regime he served as a prefect, and they soon rewarded him for his faithful service by elevating him to the peerage. Alexis de Tocqueville thus grew up in a strictly aristocratic family that held in the highest regard the traditions and ideals of the *ancien régime.* Late in life Tocqueville recalled how his family had settled in a fine Verneuil chateau and had kept company with other noble families.[2] His childhood playmates and friends were his cousins, the Chateaubriands, and he received his Catholic education from the Abbé Lesueur. Family, relatives, and friends frequently gathered about the hearth while his mother sang a famous air recounting their troubles during the Revolution and the fate of Louis XVI. When she had finished the song, everyone burst into tears, not so much over their own misfortunes and suffering as in mourning for their lost king.

Like their father, both Alexis' older brothers adopted aristocratic careers. Édouard became "a cultured and conservative seigneur" and Hyppolite entered the army, the customary career for the eldest son. Alexis attended the Lycée at Metz where he was an undistinguished student who developed little interest in books, failed the classics, and excelled only in what his dedicated tutor, Lesueur, had taught him: "the art of rhetoric and French composition." [3]

While still a young boy fifteen years of age, he discovered in his father's library some skeptical and agnostic literature, probably the work of the *philosophes,* which formed the beginning of his own serious doubts. Although he never became an atheist, the experience permanently undermined his faith. "Je crois, mais je ne puis pratiquer," he later summed up his feelings.

At eighteen, Alexis moved to Paris where, after studying law for three years, he acquired in 1827 a position in the magistracy. Soon afterward his father secured him an appointment as *juge auditeur,* a kind of apprentice magistrate, in the court at Versailles. His father, who meanwhile had become a *Comte,* was also transferred to Versailles and

---

[2] For these and other biographical details, see George Wilson Pierson's classic study, *Tocqueville and Beaumont in America* (New York: Oxford University Press, 1938), pp. 3–34; in addition consult Gustave de Beaumont's introduction to *Oeuvres et Correspondance Inédites D'Alexis de Tocqueville,* tome I (Paris: Michel Lévy Frères, 1861), pp. 3–110; and J. P. Mayer, *Alexis de Tocqueville: A Biographical Essay in Political Science* (New York: The Viking Press, 1949).

[3] Pierson, *op. cit.,* p. 17.

became an intimate companion of the king. Hervé de Tocqueville and his wife then moved in the highest circles of French society, which appeared to assure what they wanted most for the eloquent Alexis, a brilliant judicial career.

A career in law, however, is not what the young Tocqueville wanted. Although he did not quite know how to go about achieving it, he aspired to become a statesman. "Politics," as Pierson observed, ". . . was beginning to absorb his most earnest attention." [4] Observing the struggles of the liberals with the reactionary Charles X, and increasingly critical of the conservatives and their régime, Alexis became more sympathetic toward the liberal movement. He moved quite far from his family's political views — so far that he ceased to discuss politics with them. He opposed as impractical, dangerous, and foolish the efforts of Louis XVIII and Charles X to restore and reimpose the old order on contemporary French society. Pierson observed that the young man had learned to think for himself and that after considering the political discussions and debates raging at the time, began more and more to reject the royalist and aristocratic dogmas and to identify himself with the young liberals. The latter, who were mainly the disciples of Royer-Collard, "were just preparing to enter the political arena as the friends of 'liberty' and better government, the champions of a more liberal and progressive régime." [5]

Yet the young Tocqueville's liberalism was quite moderate and he had many doubts, personal as well as political. His deeply embedded aristocratic values moved him to want to serve his country, preferably as a statesman. But at the same time he perceived in himself a colossal ignorance of history, politics, and cultures other than his own, which seemed to preclude such a career. To overcome this ignorance, he decided in 1826 at age twenty to travel in Italy and Sicily with his brother Édouard. In addition, Alexis promised himself to read copiously and seriously.

During his travels, Tocqueville took notes and recorded his impressions, which resulted in two rather large manuscripts.[6] Gustave de Beaumont, whom Tocqueville met soon after returning to France and who eventually became his collaborator, lifelong friend, and editor, wrote that the young Tocqueville had no illusions about the merit and quality of the manuscripts. "[T]rès-médiocre," he wrote on the envelope containing

---

[4] *Ibid.*, p. 18.
[5] *Ibid.*, p. 20.
[6] See *Oeuvres Complètes* Vol. V, Pt. 1. Edition définitive publiée sous la direction de J. P. Mayer (Paris: Gallimard, 1951–1967).

one.[7] When Tocqueville and Beaumont first met they had much in common: both were young magistrates of noble birth, idealistic but ambitious men, and liberals — though Beaumont, three years older than Tocqueville, apparently had fewer doubts and stood more firmly in the liberal camp.

The two young men began their friendship by studying together. Some radical liberals had been saying that France was in trouble because she had not had her 1688, so Tocqueville and Beaumont felt it necessary to study English history. They also probably read some political economy by J. B. Say. Most important, however, in understanding their intellectual development is that they attended the lectures of François Guizot, who taught them that history was governed by inexorable laws. (Tocqueville described what he regarded as irresistible historical developments or social forces as "providential," just as Karl Marx spoke of the historical necessity or inevitability of particular developments.) But Guizot's most important idea was that middle-class growth was the basis of social progress. The ultimate victory of the *bourgeoisie* was inevitable. The Third Estate had destroyed both feudalism and the power of the church and now it was successfully assailing the restored monarchy.

Guizot was the most immediate source of Tocqueville's own ideas about the irresistible advance of equality and democracy, two ambiguous terms he chose never to define but which he continued nevertheless to employ throughout his works, preferring apparently to speak of these abstract ideas rather than the social classes who "carried" them. In any case, he saw Europe as being swept by a permanent democratic-equalitarian revolution. This *idée mère,* almost an *idée fixe,* dominated his thinking, his writing, and his politics all his life.

The young Tocqueville became convinced by 1830 that France was drifting toward revolution and chaos and that her leaders would make no concessions to the people to forestall the upheaval. When on July 25, 1830, Charles X had failed to obtain the support of the chamber and issued his repressive decrees, Tocqueville's worst fears materialized: uprisings in Paris, barricades, and revolution, which did not result, however, in popular rule but politically strengthened the *bourgeoisie.* Bankers, large merchants, industrialists, and their spokesmen succeeded in placing on the throne the Orleanist dynasty in the person of Louis Philippe. For Tocqueville the revolution was a vivid and concrete manifestation of the rising tide of democracy. Although France this time had

---

[7] Beaumont, *op. cit.,* pp. 4ff.

4

barely escaped popular rule, such rule remained for Tocqueville and other members of his class, including among them the most liberal and enlightened, a real and frightening eventuality. If, however, the revolutionary developments of 1830 were frightening and distasteful to Tocqueville, they were for his parents an unmitigated disaster. Their whole world collapsed with the fall of the House of Bourbon, for they would have no part of the new régime and nothing to do with Louis Philippe, whom they resented as a traitor to the Bourbon cause, a usurper who servilely accepted his power and his crown from "below," from the bourgeoisie.

Tocqueville and Beaumont also despised Louis Philippe and his alliance with the middle classes. But what were the options? Tocqueville was among those who suspected that the Bourbons would never again rule, and that for the time being restoring them to power was definitely out of the question. If therefore he supported the new régime, it was only to forestall something he saw as far worse. Explaining his motives at the time to an acquaintance, he wrote: "If Louis Philippe were overturned, it would certainly not be in favour of Henry IV, but of the republic and of anarchy. Those who love their country ought therefore to rally frankly to the new power, since it alone can now save France from herself. . . ." [8]

Tocqueville and Beaumont now swore allegiance to the new power, thereby alienating themselves from their relatives and friends, some of whom went so far as to accuse Tocqueville of cowardice, opportunism, and self-interest. The revolution had effectively split Tocqueville's family because his older brothers refused to take an oath of allegiance to the new monarchy and with their father sided with the exiled Bourbons.

Both young men now found themselves in an embarrassing and uncomfortable position because they were outcasts in their own circles without having won the confidence of the new power. If their chiefs in the former régime had regarded them warily as too liberal, their present superiors suspected them as reactionaries, surreptitiously maintaining their loyalty to the Bourbons. When his superiors required him to take the oath a second time, Tocqueville saw that rising in the magistracy to a position of real influence, as he had hoped, was quite unlikely. Moreover, great revolutionary unrest and persisting serious disorders placed

---

[8] Quoted in Pierson, *op. cit.*, p. 29. This attitude, as we shall see, not always evident in his intellectual work, remained characteristic of Tocqueville throughout his political career. As compared with what he called a "republic and anarchy," almost any regime was the lesser of two evils.

tne survival of the régime in doubt. If he remained in the country and Louis Philippe's government were indeed to fall, Tocqueville feared that by then he would have become so thoroughly identified with it as to spoil his chances with the successors. Under the circumstances, Tocqueville decided quickly to dissociate himself from those ruling at the time and, if possible, to leave France altogether. A few days after taking the oath a second time Tocqueville, with Beaumont who shared his assessment of the situation, requested permission to study prison reforms in the United States.

Such a mission, they apparently reasoned, would enable them to escape their discomfort and to solve both their personal and their professional problems. By the time they completed their mission the fate of the July Monarchy would have been settled. Regardless of whether it fell or consolidated itself, the two young men would be able to take prominent positions in the chamber "as masters of one of the new liberal reforms, leaders in the cause that had not yet become involved in party politics, but appealed to the sympathies of all. In short, the prison mission would be for them the ladder to a new career, the first step toward influence and fame." [9] Also, of course, the mission provided an opportunity to see the American republic — the very form of government whose establishment Tocqueville feared most in his own country. "I have long had the greatest desire," he wrote to a friend in August 1830, "to visit North America: I shall go see there what a great republic is like; my only fear is lest, during that time they establish one in France. . . ." [10]

Tocqueville definitely planned to write a fine book on America that would win him public attention and acclaim. In addition, a study of a society in which, as he believed, democracy and equality had won out would give the Frenchmen of his social class an idea of the direction in which French society appeared inexorably to be moving and, perhaps, an idea of how they might turn the inevitable to their advantage. Not a republic but a constitutional monarchy, based on the Bourbons, and combining the principle of representation with the authority of the Prince, would best accomplish this and at the same time preserve liberty — another key term Tocqueville chose never to define.[11]

Their minds made up, all that remained for the young men was to persuade their superiors of the importance of the projected mission by pointing out the backwardness of the prison system in France, the need

[9] *Ibid.*, p. 31.
[10] Quoted in *ibid.*
[11] Beaumont, *op. cit.*, pp. 11ff.

for reform, and the fact that the most advanced form of experimentation, the penitentiary system, was to be found in the United States. After numerous difficulties and some three months of negotiation in which their respective families intervened in their behalf, the government granted them leave but not the financial aid they had hoped for to defray expenses. This setback was only temporary; for in the end, their families agreed, despite political differences, to provide the necessary funds. Equipped with money, letters of introduction and credit, books about the United States, Say's economic text, a prayer book received as a gift from the Abbé Lesueur, and their credentials as government commissioners, they left for Havre, sailed for thirty-eight days, and arrived in New York on May 12, 1831.

By coincidence, the two young Frenchmen, already heavily preoccupied with what they regarded as the rising tide of "democracy," arrived in the United States just at the moment when the antithesis, aristocracy-democracy, appeared to be a very lively public issue. Of course, aristocracy in the American context referred not to a hereditary landed nobility, but rather to the large, rich property holders. The issue, as the Jacksonians saw it, was "whether People, or Property, shall govern? Democracy implies a government by the people. . . . Aristocracy implies a government of the rich." [12] Given this atmosphere with the ideas he held so firmly about democracy and the equalitarian ideals he encountered in the United States that so sharply contrasted with his own aristocratic values, it is no wonder that Tocqueville perceived almost everything in terms of the dichotomous principles, aristocracy-democracy. Nor is it any wonder that the struggle between these principles, and the irresistible movement from one to the other as the basis of social organization, became the master theme of his first book and most of his subsequent works as well.

---

[12] These words of the fiery Jacksonian senator, Thomas Hart Benton, were quoted in Arthur M. Schlesinger, Jr., *The Age of Jackson* (Boston: Little, Brown, 1946), p. 125.

I. Tocqueville and America

1. Democracy in America

IN HIS FIRST MAJOR WORK, Tocqueville wrote of America but thought of his own country. In America, he believed, the *demos* ruled in its unadulterated state. Yet, much of what he strongly desired for France he found in America: order, a government based on the separation and balance of powers, true liberty. And the phenomena he despised and feared in France were nonexistent in American society.

For Tocqueville, the important thing about America was that she had had her democratic revolution and yet had managed to escape France's fate — "anarchy" alternating with despotism. The rule of the French people appeared inevitable. How then should the French elite adapt to this with the least pain? He hoped America could provide some guidelines — especially because she appeared to Tocqueville as a post-revolutionary, middle-class society in which democracy had largely won out. This conception led Tocqueville to treat America as a predominantly one-class or "classless" society in which the democratic revolution had completed much of its work; all forms of inequality, including social classes, were disappearing, while greater and greater equality was becoming the rule.

This view led to mistakes, not only with regard to America but England and France as well. For Tocqueville treated as *exceptional* all phenomena that did not fit into his general scheme. He minimized or missed altogether the socio-historical significance of urbanization and industrialization and the new social classes accompanying these processes. Tocqueville's conception, which led him to accentuate some aspects of American social structure and to minimize others, and the errors this caused him to make, will be taken up later in this study. Presently, however, it must be emphasized that the same "one-sidedness" of his model brought a certain gain; it helped Tocqueville grasp and bring into relief the predominantly middle-class character of American society and culture.

America, Tocqueville observed, had never had an old régime, nor a protracted and violent struggle between it and the middle classes; it had no centralized state bureaucracy, no great metropolitan areas, and, finally, no great industrial centers. For Tocqueville, the absence of these conditions, to mention only the internal conditions, made the American form of order and liberty possible. America, as he saw it, was one great, relatively homogeneous, agrarian middle class, with the extremes of wealth and poverty having no real social or historical significance. Under the influence of his general theory, then, Tocqueville accentuated equality in America; equality was the fundamental consequence of the democratic revolution from which all else was derived. In Europe, too, one could see democracy and equality "rapidly rising into power." A great universal democratic revolution was gathering momentum every day. Indeed, one meaning of "democracy," for Tocqueville, was the historical ascendancy of the middle and lower orders to prominence and power. These orders, particularly the commercial classes, had been gaining increasingly in both economic and political power. Ultimately this process in France had led to the dissolution and collapse of the old régime. The foundations of the new, however, seemed no less vulnerable than those of the old. In the new system capitalists were gaining hegemony but appeared no more secure before their "underclass" than were the feudal lords in the face of the rising bourgeoisie. To Tocqueville, then, democracy and equality described the apparently permanent and inexorable revolution of the lower classes. "Can it be believed," he asked, "that the democracy which has overthrown the feudal system and vanquished kings will retreat before tradesmen and capitalists?" [1] The irresistible character of this revolution prompted him to describe it as providential, as the will of God. In addition, this was perhaps a useful figure with which to counter the ultraconservatives who regarded every departure from the old order as a violation of the divine will.

Irresistible and providential though it was, the revolutionary process

---

[1] Alexis de Tocqueville, *Democracy in America,* the Henry Reeve text, revised by Frances Bowen, and further corrected and edited with an introduction, editorial notes, and bibliographies, by Phillip Bradley (New York: Knopf, 1948). Page references to Volume I of this work will hereafter appear in parentheses immediately following the quoted passage.

nonetheless required the guidance of men; guidance, in turn, required knowledge: "A new science of politics is needed for a new world" (7). The great social revolution in France "has always advanced without guidance," which largely accounted for the violently convulsive crises in that country as opposed to the relatively peaceful and gradual character of change in England and America. The powerful, intelligent, and moral classes of France never controlled the process but left it in the hands of the lower orders, with their "wild instincts." In France "democracy has grown up like those children who have no parental guidance. . . ." The French upper classes had failed historically to make the lower fit to govern, which would have required sharing power. Instead "all were bent on excluding [the people] from the government" (8). For this reason — Tocqueville here directed his argument to the members of his class — democracy has been perceived as evil and the benefits it might confer, ignored.

Democracy, Tocqueville argued, clearly brings with it certain losses for a minority but definite gains for the majority. With democracy, if properly guided, "comfort would be more general" and "ignorance would be less common." At the same time the likelihood of violent disorder, conflict, or despotism would diminish. However, the people's revolution in France has remained unguided, with the result that hostility among classes has increased, despite the fact that the actual distance between rich and poor is not so great as it was; the central government has gathered unto itself the powers of the various secondary groups destroyed by the Revolution; and, finally, as religion has identified and allied itself with the anti-democratic forces, democracy has virtually destroyed religion, totally rejecting even its moral elements essential to order.

In one country, however, democracy has not been accompanied by these consequences. Quite the contrary, it is "reaping the fruits of the democratic revolution," without, however, paying the terrible costs Tocqueville's countrymen had paid and were continuing to pay. Thus Tocqueville began to fashion his image of democracy in America — a democracy flourishing under optimal conditions.

More than once during his intellectual development, Tocqueville acknowledged the influence of English history and institutions on his thinking. Soon after the publication of *Democracy,* which was greeted in his own country with great enthusiasm, he wrote to Nassau W. Senior that pleased though he was with the book's success in France, "I shall not be satisfied unless it extends to what I consider, in an intellectual sense, my second country." [2] And many years later, in 1851, he wrote similarly: "I care almost as much about what is said of me on your side of the Channel as I do for what is said of me on ours. So many of my opinions and feelings are English, that England is to me almost a second country intellectually." [3]

Tocqueville found English social and political experiences important because England had succeeded in preserving the aristocratic form of liberty, which he much preferred to the republican form. England had achieved a conspicuous degree of liberty while preserving her aristocracy, and had prevented excessive centralization of government as well as violent class conflicts resulting in violent insurrections. So great was the intellectual influence of Tocqueville's "second country" that he even attributed much of the success of democracy in America to the English origin of her earliest settlers.

The English brought to America that fruitful germ of free institutions, the township. The social background of those who laid down the economic, political, and religious foundations of the new society was, significantly, strictly middle class. From the beginning the social background of the settlers militated against forming a landed aristocracy. Free farmers, each with his small private plot, worked a land that seemed to demand the self-interested efforts of the owner himself.

On this social basis, there emerged in America not the aristocratic form of liberty of the mother country but rather ". . . that freedom of the middle and lower orders of which the history of the world had as yet furnished no complete example" (29). In the North, and particularly in New England, most settlers had an independent, middle-class background. They shared religion, language, and even political creed, as well as class origin. They were Puritan, middle class, capitalistic, and democratic — a configuration to which Tocqueville returned several times.

Long before Max Weber reflected on the question, Tocqueville observed in what he called Anglo-American civilization two distinct elements: the *spirit of religion* and the *spirit of liberty,* to which he later added a third, the *spirit of commerce.* Speaking of the settlers of New England, he observes: "One sees them . . . seeking with almost equal eagerness material wealth and moral satisfaction; heaven in the world

[2] *Correspondence and Conversations of Alexis de Tocqueville with Nassau William Senior,* vol. I edited by M. C. M. Simpson (London: Henry S. King, 1872), p. 5.
[3] *Ibid.,* p. 264.

beyond, and well-being and liberty in this one" (43). The middle-class make-up of the bulk of the early immigration caused a social homogeneity that tended to preclude class conflict. Tocqueville also recognized that the middle-class emigration "removed the elements of fresh discord and further revolutions" in the country of origin — England.

For Tocqueville, America's democratic institutions were most "perfect" in New England, where the people directed their own public affairs and voted their own taxes. And though Tocqueville was not blind to the negative, constraining side of these communities, notably the "narrow sectarian spirit" of the Puritanical laws, he emphasized what he most admired about them: "personal liberty," "trial by jury," and "the responsibility of the agents of power." These laws were made possible not only by the common background, but particularly by "an almost perfect equality of fortune, and a still greater uniformity of opinions" (39).

The independent township was the "life and mainspring of American liberty"; it was the "nucleus round which the local interests, passions, rights and duties collected and clung . . ." (40). In contrast with European society, whose political organization began with the superior ranks, American society (New England) was constituted from the bottom up — and this had taken place precisely when absolutism triumphed on the Continent.

If the condition of the Anglo-Americans was highly equalitarian, it was due in large part to the absence of a great, firmly entrenched, landed aristocracy. This was a very important fact to Tocqueville as it meant that in America, unlike France and other European countries, the democratic principle could prevail without the prolonged and painful process of destroying the older order. But democracy had not triumphed in America without struggle or revolution. The colonies had something of an aristocracy, so that the rebellion against the mother country, the war for independence, became simultaneously a *social* revolution. Tocqueville wrote:

> Intelligence in New England and wealth in the country to the south of the Hudson long exercised a sort of aristocratic influence, which tended to keep the exercise of social power in the hands of a few. . . .
> The American Revolution broke out, and the doctrine of the sovereignty of the people came out of the townships and took possession of the state . . . (56).

What impressed Tocqueville most about the political-administrative structure of American society was its extreme degree of decentralization, especially as compared with France. So great was the autonomy of the states that the Union appeared to be composed of "twenty-four small sovereign nations." As for municipal autonomy, that fundamental principle of liberty, it too was very much alive in America. The importance of this principle Tocqueville emphasized in all his major works. In this work he noted painfully that the European nations, his own country included, no longer experienced its advantages. Tocqueville understood that if the political principle of municipal freedom in America allowed the people to remain the masters of their representatives, this was made possible by the relative social and economic equality that prevailed in the community. If in political life the elected officials had not transformed themselves from servants into masters, this was related to the fact that there was no marked development of masters and servants in social and economic life.

Tocqueville continually highlights these contrasts between America and France. His praise of local autonomy and decentralization in America may be read as a critique of the centralized state bureaucracy in France — a phenomenon to which he devoted much attention in his final work, *The Old Regime and the French Revolution.* Already here in his *Democracy,* however, he saw the profound differences it made for political life when the community was rent into mutually hostile classes as in France, and when it was not, as in America — although, as we shall later see, Tocqueville greatly exaggerated the relative absence of social stratification in America and mistook the absence of an old order for the absence of any social classes whatsoever. "In New England," he wrote, "no tradition exists of a distinction of rank; no portion of the community is tempted to oppress the remainder; and the wrongs that may injure isolated individuals are forgotten in the general contentment that prevails" (68). Correspondingly, administration was invisible in America, especially hierarchical administration.

Later, in his *Old Regime,* he will demonstrate that the centralized state bureaucracy, contrary to what was commonly believed at the time, long antedated the French Revolution and was in fact a legacy of the old order. Clearly, then, the absence of such an order, and its struggles with the new, would largely account for the comparative absence of a centralized and oppressive administration in America. In addition, of course, much weight had to be given to the favorable birthplace of American democracy:

> The Americans have no neighbors and consequently they have no great wars, or financial crises, or inroads, or conquest to dread; they require

neither great taxes, nor large armies, nor great generals; and they have nothing to fear from a scourge which is more formidable to republics than all these evils combined; namely, military glory (289).

These factors contributed in America to the relatively unobtrusive and unoppressive character of the state.

An important distinction was to be made between "Centralized government" and "centralized administration." The first referred to the concentration of power that seemed necessary to watch over and attend to the nation's general interests. On the other hand, when concentrated power directed and interfered with the interests and affairs of local communities, this could be regarded as centralized administration. In both America and England there was great centralization of government but not of administration; no great centralized hierarchy of public functionaries existed. Throughout *Democracy,* his praise of decentralization is polemical, directed against the partisans in his own country of the highly centralized state. What emerges, however, is a critique of bureaucracy in general. What he had seen in his own country persuaded him that however it might begin, a centralized bureaucracy eventually becomes the absolute master of liberty and life:

> Centralization imparts without difficulty an admirable regularity to the routine of business; provides skillfully for the details of the social police; represses small disorders and petty misdemeanors; maintains society in a *status quo* alike secure from improvement and decline; and perpetuates a drowsy regularity in the conduct of affairs which the heads of the administration are wont to call good order and public tranquility; in short it excels in prevention, but not in action (90).

What, in contrast, did one see in America, where the administration was "far less regular, less enlightened, and less skillful"? There the people had done what was required by and for themselves. Political decentralization had allowed for unfettered individual initiative and private enterprise. Yet in no other country did the people "make such exertions for the common weal" (91).

Thus the American form of liberty rested on the preservation and development of autonomous local and provincial institutions. Every nation requires such institutions but a democratic nation especially requires them. For when such institutions are severely weakened, as was the case in France, the nation fails to strike the proper balance that successfully avoids two extreme evils: anarchy on the one hand or despotism on the other. "Those who dread the license of the mob," he writes, "and those who fear absolute power ought alike to desire the gradual development of provincial liberties."

Reflecting particularly on France, Tocqueville argues that democracies are especially vulnerable to a centralized despotism because they lack organized, local powers capable of resisting a despot. Thus as the central authority gathers unto itself virtually all power, nothing stands between it and the unorganized, atomized, and hence powerless populace, which then can be intimidated at will. This special vulnerability of democracies has been overlooked by those who support as a bulwark of freedom the centralized state, a result of the French Revolution.[4] A more careful and critical scrutiny reveals, however, that two contradictory tendencies in the revolution ought not to be confused: "The one was favorable to liberty, the other to despotism."

If the preservation of provincial and local autonomy as organic, almost "natural" checks against centralized despotism was an essential condition of liberty, so was the development of political checks and balances, constitutionalism, and other political safeguards. Tocqueville united both principles in his theory of good government, for only both together could prevent the domination of the whole people from the center. A plurality of relatively autonomous *social* bases of power was as essential as carefully defining and separating the power and responsibility of the respective branches of government — the executive, legislative, and judicial. Separation of powers in this double sense appeared real and effective in the United States without, however, having weakened in the least what Tocqueville called "centralized government," i.e., government attending to the general interests of the nation. This, again, stood out in contrast to France, where both principles had been seriously undermined, almost destroyed, and where the central government had been weakened besides.

Among the branches of government in the United States, the organization of the judicial power appeared unique. Its main general characteristics were, first, that it tended to arbitrate not only between the other branches but also between the state and federal governments. Second, it pronounced on special cases, not on general principles; and, finally, it acted only when called upon. The American judge had more power than one

---

[4] During his research for *The Old Regime and the French Revolution,* to be considered in the final part of the present study, Tocqueville discovered that centralized administration was *not* an innovation of the revolution and that it had only continued and accentuated what had begun much earlier under the old order.

would at first have supposed; he could check the other branches without, however, weakening their respective powers.

What impressed Tocqueville greatly was the fact that judicial decisions were founded on the Constitution, and not simply on laws. The judge had the power to declare some laws unconstitutional, and in this way to prevent them from being applied; the more often this occurred, the more a specific law lost its moral force. On the other hand, because the judge could not intervene without being invited to do so, the system was quite favorable to liberty. Thus within the limits imposed, the power of the American courts of justice to declare a statute unconstitutional "forms one of the most powerful barriers that have ever been devised against the tyranny of political assemblies" (103).

Another important characteristic of the American system was its carefully defined political jurisdiction not only in general but with respect to public officials. For although it was true that in both Europe and the United States one branch of the legislature "is authorized to impeach and the other to judge," there was nevertheless a great difference between the European and American systems: in Europe the political tribunals tried and punished the offender, but in America they could only deprive him of his official rank. Then their jurisdiction ended and that of the ordinary courts began. This applied even to the highest official in the land. An impeached president had to be "tried by a jury, which alone . . . [could] deprive him of liberty or life" (107). "The principal object of the political tribunals of Europe is to punish the offender; of those in America, to deprive him of his power" (110).

Tocqueville remained ambivalent, however, toward this system. It seemed to prevent the worst forms of legislative tyranny but perhaps not tyranny itself: ". . . I am not sure that political jurisdiction, as it is constituted in the United States, is not, all things considered, the most formidable weapon that has ever been placed in the grasp of a majority. When the American republics begin to degenerate, it will be easy to verify the truth of this observation by remarking whether the number of political impeachments is increased" (111). For Tocqueville, the degeneration of the republic resulting in a tyranny of the majority was a likely development — one much to be feared.

POLITICAL PARTIES IN A "CLASSLESS" SOCIETY

It is quite clear that Tocqueville viewed the United States as an essentially classless society or at the very least as a society well on the way to such a condition. In his view there did not exist in the United States anything like the situations in France or England: classes of people living under such fundamentally unequal circumstances that it was almost as if they were two nations instead of one. And in any case whatever inequalities existed in America would not survive for long. Tocqueville recognized that in certain other societies basic inequalities lead to a condition in which the separate classes "have contradictory interests, and . . . may consequently be in a perpetual state of opposition" (174). Sometimes these conflicts of interest lead only to political changes; at other times, the conflict is deeper and "the existence of society itself is endangered. Such are the times of great revolutions and of great parties" (174). The "great parties" that lead and direct the conflicts are great because of the genuineness of their convictions and the boldness of their conduct: "In them private interest, which always plays the chief part in political passions, is more studiously veiled under the pretext of the public good; and it may even be sometimes concealed from the eyes of the very persons whom it excites and impels" (175).

If in times of revolution great parties arise and come to the fore, they decline with the calm that succeeds the revolution and are displaced by small parties that are "deficient in political good faith," "less dignified by lofty purposes," and obviously more narrowly selfish. America, "has had great parties, but has them no longer . . ." (175). After the War of Independence the main conflict revolved about one social issue: whether to extend or limit the power of the people; the struggle between the two major parties did in some degree reflect this issue. But the basic class homogeneity of the society assured that in neither of the two parties "were a great number of private interests affected by success or defeat . . ." (176).

If anything now threatened the integrity of the Union, it was not class but regional conflicts over material interests. "The parties by which the Union is menaced do not rest upon principles, but upon material interests. These interests constitute, in the different provinces of so vast an empire, rival nations rather than parties. Thus upon a recent occasion the North contended for the system of commercial prohibition, and the South took up arms in favor of free trade, simply because the North is a manufacturing and the South an agricultural community; and the restrictive system that was profitable to the one was prejudicial to the other" (177). Here, we see that Tocqueville perceived the distinct economic bases of the respective regions; but he did not see the inevitable growth and preponderance of capitalist industry in the North and the new classes and conflicts accompanying it. The main forms of social conflict in the future were to be sectional and regional.

The more Tocqueville studied the numerous small parties in existence at the time, the more he perceived that they reflected not a simple diversification of interests but a dichotomy. Most parties, he observed, "are more or less connected with one or the other of those two great divisions which have always existed in free communities. The deeper we penetrate into the inmost thought of these parties, the more we perceive that the object of the one is to limit and that of the other to extend the authority of the people" (178). Jacksonian America seemed to validate his theory that that country had entered its post-revolutionary, increasingly democratic-equalitarian phase. The poorer classes had won out in America and "the more affluent classes . . . have no influence in political affairs . . ." (179). Tocqueville continued to hold firmly to this view. In America there were "rich" and "poor" only in a very relative sense. In this "classless" situation parties nevertheless fought one another and employed "two chief weapons": newspapers and public associations.

FREEDOM OF THE PRESS AND PUBLIC ASSOCIATIONS

Although Tocqueville was as ambivalent about the guarantees of the first amendment as he was on many others, he tended to argue more often than not that the only alternative to freedom of the press, speech, and assembly was despotism. He would have preferred an intermediate position "between the complete independence and the entire servitude of opinion" but could discover no such tenable one. History had shown that what began as an effort merely to prevent the abuses of liberty ended in its destruction. To avoid servitude one must tolerate what he called the abuse of liberty, or license: "in order," he writes, "to enjoy the inestimable benefits that the liberty of the press ensures, it is necessary to submit to the inevitable evils that it creates" (184).

As for the violent tone and openly abusive language employed by the modern press, these were every bit as characteristic of the American press as of the French — perhaps more so. Those of his countrymen who attributed the "violence of the press" to the instability of the social condition and to the intensity of the social conflicts were probably in error. America, after all, "contains the fewest germs of revolution"; but the press in that country does not employ a less violent and abusive tone than it does in France. This tone, however, exists in America for different reasons.

For the Americans, freedom of the press was a very old and real liberty. But its influence was necessarily limited by the structure of the society and by "material interests." "In America political life is active, varied, even agitated, but is rarely affected by those deep passions which are excited only when material interests are impaired; and in the United States these interests are prosperous. . . . In America three quarters of the enormous sheet are filled with advertisements, and the remainder is frequently occupied by political intelligence or trivial anecdotes; it is only from time to time that one finds a corner devoted to passionate discussions like those which the journalists of France every day give to their readers" (185). In France newspapers were class organs; in America they were not. But there were still other reasons for the apparently limited influence of the American press, which also could best be understood by contrasting its situation with that of France.

In France, the press is highly centralized in a double sense: it is centered in Paris, and in a few hands. The press thus becomes an enormously influential force. In America, in contrast, the absence of a central metropolis and the existence of a wide diffusion of innumerable newspapers, precludes the concentration of influence. Moreover, it is precisely the very large number of periodicals that tends to diminish their influence, by canceling one another out as it were. The Americans, then, neither use nor need censorship to control the press for "it is an axiom of political science in that country that the only way to neutralize the effect of the public journals is to multiply their number" (186). Thus, although in France the power of the press can pit class against class and the people against the government, the power of the press in America takes a different form for it is as decentralized as the other major institutions, notably the economic and political. This does not mean that the struggle in America between the people and the aristocracy has ceased; on the contrary, it is an ever-present phenomenon, and reflected in the press: "All the political journals of the United States," wrote Tocqueville, "are, indeed, arrayed on the side of the administration or against it; but they attack and defend it in a thousand different ways. They cannot form those great currents of opinion which sweep away the strongest dikes" (186). This corresponds to the relatively homogeneous social condition: without great class differences, the struggle prevails over innumerable small matters; and without a centralized power dominating all and everything, the struggle is localized.

In addition, the newspaper in America was a predominantly commercial venture — a "commodity." The press appealed to the lowest common denominator and employed a "coarse appeal to the passions" of the readers, not primarily to impel them to act on certain issues but to sell newspapers.

ASSOCIATIONS

The Americans, Tocqueville observed, formed many associations for many purposes. Associations are two-edged, for they serve as an important instrument of democracy but also as a "guarantee against the tyranny of the majority" (194). Associations are potentially dangerous popular instruments. But in America, on balance, associations are perhaps less so since they tend to fragment the majority. Tocqueville therefore views associations and their proliferation in much the same manner as he does the press: the incredibly large number of associations creates a situation in which they neutralize one another. Acting in a multitude of groups, formed to achieve a multitude of objects, tends to prevent the people from banding together to form an omnipotent majority.

Associations in America had to be viewed in the context of the social homogeneity and political decentralization that he believed was characteristic of early nineteenth-century American society. In the absence of great class schisms and, consequently, violent class conflicts, the Americans did not regard association, as did most Frenchmen, "as a weapon which is to be hastily fashioned and immediately tried in conflict" (196). Neither was association a means of mobilizing an army "to march against the enemy"; nor did freedom of association mean, exclusively, the "right of attacking the government" (197). Rather, political associations in America, where "differences of opinion are mere differences of hue," were formed to check the majority or win it over to one's side, but always by strictly legal and peaceable means.

THE VARIOUS SIDES OF DEMOCRACY

To Tocqueville, democracy appeared to have gained the upper hand in America, and without a long and costly struggle. To whom could this fact be more vitally important "than to the [members of the] French nation, who are blindly driven onwards, by a daily and irresistible impulse, towards a state of things which may prove either despotic or republican, but which will assuredly be democratic . . ." (199)? Here as elsewhere one sees the ambiguous sense in which Tocqueville used the term "democracy," reflecting his fundamental ambivalence. All democracies are

23

potentially despotic. Tocqueville's thesis here elaborates an ancient idea and, on the other hand, also anticipates the substance of what later thinkers, such as Pareto, Mosca, and Michels, would argue.

Men in all societies must labor in order to live, and although subsistence is more easily acquired in some societies than in others, most people in all societies will be "forced to work in order to procure the means of subsistence. . . . It is therefore quite as difficult to imagine a state in which all the citizens are very well informed as a state in which they are all wealthy . . ." (200). Hence, the perennial incompetence of the masses. Having neither the time nor the means to study and examine the important issues rationally and carefully, the people's "conclusions are hastily formed from a superficial inspection of the more prominent features of a question. Hence it often happens that mountebanks of all sorts are able to please the people, while their truest friends frequently fail to gain their confidence" (201). For these and other reasons a democracy may degenerate.

Moreover, because the masses are today universally agitated, restless, and impatient, possessing "a passion for equality which they can never entirely satisfy"; and because any manifestation of superiority is "irksome in their sight," they are destined never to be sated and always disappointed. All this heightens the probability that in crises, they will turn to charlatans and demagogues. And if the United States had been spared this fate, it was to be largely attributed to the absence in that country of classes and class hatred. Even America, however, despite its favorable conditions, will require the injection of certain "aristocratic" principles. Tocqueville therefore called for indirect election "or run the risk of perishing miserably among the shoals of democracy"; of equal importance will be the creation of an aristocratic stratum of unpaid public officers.

For Tocqueville it was a "fixed rule" that societies are always divided into at least three classes: the rich, the well-off, and the poor. The good society moderated the conflicts of interest among the three classes. The good society required good government: a system that assured both order and liberty and effected the appropriate synthesis of aristocratic and democratic principles.

What were the advantages and disadvantages of the two principles? Aristocracies tend to "work for themselves and not for the people" (235). Nevertheless, the aristocratic principle is definitely superior to both the monarchical and democratic: the king may err, vacillate, or be biased; he is, after all, only one mortal. The masses, on the other hand, can be "led astray by ignorance and passion." "But an aristocratic body," Tocqueville concluded, "is too numerous to be led astray by intrigue, and yet not numerous enough to yield readily to the intoxication of unreflecting passion. An aristocracy is a firm and enlightened body that never dies" (236).

The advantage of democracy is that it promotes the welfare of the greatest number. This is as undeniable as the fact that aristocracies tend to concentrate wealth and power in a few hands. In an aristocracy it is essential that the leaders govern with ability and honesty, for lacking these qualities it has lost its main virtues. These qualities are also important in a democracy but even more important is that the interests of leaders and led should coincide. Shared interests are more easily assured in a democracy, because the people not only have a better understanding of their own interests but also have the power to depose those who are inattentive to their interests or who act against them. However, some conflict between those who govern and those who are governed is as inevitable as the division of society into classes. Tocqueville writes:

> No political form has hitherto been discovered that is equally favorable to the prosperity and the development of all the classes into which society is divided. These classes continue to form, as it were, so many distinct communities in the same nation; and experience has shown that it is no less dangerous to place the fate of these classes exclusively in the hands of any one of them than it is to make one people the arbiter of the destiny of another. When the rich alone govern, the interest of the poor is always endangered; and when the poor make the laws, that of the rich incurs very serious risks. The advantage of democracy does not consist, therefore, as has sometimes been asserted, in favoring the prosperity of all, but simply in contributing to the well-being of the greatest number (239).

In the United States, however, which Tocqueville viewed as a predominantly one-class society, it followed that "public officers have no class interests to promote, [and] the general and constant influence of the government is beneficial, although the individuals who conduct it are frequently unskillful and sometimes contemptible" (241). But this was unique, for the class interests in politics were obvious elsewhere. The interests of aristocratic governments are distinct from those of the majority, for "aristocracies are often carried away by their class spirit."

Even England, whose aristocracy he so much admired as honorable and enlightened, revealed that some benefited more than others from its "aristocratic liberty" and, in fact, that the others had as little liberty as they had equality.

> It cannot escape observation . . . that in the legislation of England the interests of the poor have often been sacrificed to the advantages of the rich, and the rights of the majority to the privileges of a few. The result is that England at the present day combines the extremes of good and evil fortune in the bosom of her society; and the miseries and privations of her poor almost equal her power and renown (241).

Therefore, a democracy, despite its defects, has a "secret tendency" that works for the well-being of the greatest number — just as an aristocracy, despite its virtues, tends "to contribute to the evils that oppress their fellow creatures" (241).

In America, then, it was not to be wondered at if men had a respect for right and authority. "Property," which was rapidly becoming *the social* issue in Europe, was no issue at all "in America where there are no paupers. As everyone has property of his own to defend, everyone recognizes the principle upon which he holds it" (245). But, of course, there were paupers in America and not everyone had property. Thus when Tocqueville speaks this way or asserts, similarly, that the "whole" people participated in the political process, he means the whole minus "slaves, servants, and paupers" (247), all of whom he banishes from his *Democracy* as a matter of course. When he says that the "poor rule," he means this only in a very relative sense: the middle and lower strata of the great middle class. Tocqueville does eventually turn his attention to those "below," e.g. slaves, paupers, and industrial workers; but even when he related to them with compassion, as in the case of the slaves, he leaves them permanently outside the pale of democracy.

THE THREE RACES OF THE UNITED STATES

There is perhaps no better evidence of Tocqueville's humanistic outlook than his rejection of racism in the chapters on the blacks and the Indians of the United States. But additional evidence may be found in his lengthy correspondence with his friend, Count Gobinau. The latter, as is well known, had sought in four copious volumes to demonstrate the thesis implicit in the title of his work: *The Inequality of Human Races*. This work, in turn, later exercised a great influence, through H. S. Chamberlain, on the Nazi racial theorists.

To Tocqueville, the races appeared "distinct" not so much as a result of their outward characteristics as of their education and culture. Both Indians and Negroes had been forced into inferior positions and both suffered from tyranny, and worse, at the hands of the white men. The whites oppressed the members of the other races; those they could not subdue they destroyed.

None of the dehumanizing consequences of slavery escaped Tocqueville's notice: the Negroes were deprived of all "privileges of humanity"; of their historic memories; of something as fundamental as the family; and of their language and customs without, however, having acquired "any claim to European privileges" (332). The Negro appeared, under the circumstances, to have resigned himself to his condition, servilely imitating his masters and even viewing himself through their eyes, thereby becoming "ashamed of his own nature."

Similarly, the tragic disorders European tyranny had caused among the Indians did not escape Tocqueville. The Indians rejected white culture, and their pride condemned them to death. They had been forced from their native lands, and their whole way of life was undermined and destroyed; and those who did not die of actual starvation, or at the hands of the white settlers, were reduced to begging alms. Those, finally who, acquiescing, moved from their native habitat, encountered other tribes, who met them with jealous hostility. With great human feeling, Tocqueville described the tragedy of these people, assuring his reader that he was not "coloring the picture too highly." Tribe after tribe was expelled from its land in a "regular" and "legal manner" and in this way "the Americans obtain, at a very low price, whole provinces, which the richest sovereigns of Europe could not purchase" (341). There could be no doubt that despite the virtuous and high-minded rhetoric of official policy, its main object and result was expulsion. "The rapacity of the settlers is usually backed by the tyranny of the government" (350). Moreover, the federal government and that of the separate states were "alike deficient in good faith." Time after time they broke their treaties with the Indian tribes. Seldom did Tocqueville adopt the ironic tone he used here.

As for slavery and its implications, Tocqueville remarked prophetically: "The most formidable of all the ills that threaten the future of the Union arises from the presence of a black population upon its territory, and in contemplating the cause of the present embarrassments, or the future dangers of the United States, the observer is invariably led to this as a primary fact" (356). And later, in Volume II of *Democracy,* he states the same proposition even more straightforwardly: "If ever

America undergoes great revolutions, they will be brought about by the presence of the black race on the soil of the United States; that is to say, they will owe their origin . . . to the inequality of condition" (256).

Throughout, one is impressed with Tocqueville's sensitive grasp of the black man's condition. He observed how different in its consequences was slavery in the United States as compared with the slavery of antiquity, where master and slave were of the same color and where the latter was often superior to his master in education and culture. To confer freedom upon a slave it was enough to enfranchise him, for he carried no permanent sign of his formerly servile status. In the United States, in contrast, even when a slave was set free, he could never shed the "mark of his ignominy" and inevitably transmitted it "to all his descendants." In America there was so much more "to conquer than the mere fact of servitude: the prejudice of the master, the prejudice of the race, and the prejudice of color" (358).

Tocqueville also perceived that prejudice was often stronger in the North than in the South. Where the Negroes lived formally as freemen, as they did in the North where they had no official servile status, white men shunned them lest they "be confounded together." And wherever slavery was abolished it was "not for the good of the Negroes, but for that of the Whites."

But there were still other, far-reaching and general consequences of slavery. Almost like a controlled experiment, the great differences between the border states Kentucky and Ohio demonstrated that it was precisely the institution of slavery that retarded economic development in the slave states. Slavery destroyed the dignity of labor and was uneconomical in many instances. Thus Tocqueville saw how the presence or absence of this pivotal relationship, master-slave, and its accompanying economic system, had much to do with the fact that relatively speaking the North had developed commercially and industrially while the South had not. Moreover, the differences were perpetuated by the fact that European immigrants went only to the free states, because they feared a country where labor had no honor. For the Negro, however, formal emancipation and residence in the North made little difference: he continued to perform his labor in the meanest and most degrading status. Tocqueville sensed the coming crisis and predicted "the most horrible of civil wars" (379). In the United States, and perhaps elsewhere as well, Tocqueville believed, black and white could never live together as equals and certainly not without conflict.

Moreover, though he was, like many other French notables of the time, a sincere and committed abolitionist, when the issue of abolition arose with respect to France's colonies, Tocqueville wanted definite limits imposed on the independence of the formally emancipated black man. In a speech in 1839 to the French Chamber of Deputies, Tocqueville said:

> If it be thought necessary to the cultivation of colonial produce, and to the continuation of the white race in the Antilles, that the services of the enfranchised Negro may be permanently hired by the great proprietors of the soil, it is evident that we should not create for him a domain, where he can easily live by laboring for himself alone.[5]

Thus French colonial interests took precedence over equality and freedom. But a discussion of Tocqueville's values must await a further exploration of his ideas and observations.

---

[5] Quoted in Seymour Drescher, *Dilemmas of Democracy* (Pittsburgh: University of Pittsburgh Press, 1968), p. 180.

2. Democratic Society

THE CONCEPT OF DEMOCRACY

Tocqueville used the term "democracy" in several different but related senses. First, as we have seen, it referred to the historical ascendancy, in modern times, of the so-called "lower orders," and to the social and political system in which these orders gained prominence and hegemony. Although it is not always clear whom he includes in this category, "lower orders" appears most often to refer to the middle classes and occasionally to the propertyless masses. In America, however, he largely ignored the propertyless. Given, on the one hand, Tocqueville's model of American society in which urban-industrial conditions had no long-range sociohistorical significance; and on the other, the absence of such older classes as the landed aristocracy and peasants common to Europe, his analysis unavoidably centered on the great agrarian classes, and only secondarily on commercial middle classes. America was for him a unique social order, eminently "democratic" and based predominantly if not exclusively on middle-class interests, activities, values, and institutions. But the term "democratic" in this sense could be applied, if not equally then to a large degree, to certain European societies, notably France.

It becomes especially evident, therefore, in the second volume (1840) of Tocqueville's work on America, that his model of democratic society was based not on America alone but rather on a fusion of elements abstracted from both America and France. With these elements, he fashioned a social-psychological portrait of middle-class society and culture — a portrait that bears some resemblance to Marx's conception of bourgeois values and ideology. But the resemblance must be regarded as quite superficial because when one carefully compares Tocqueville and Marx in this regard the differences become larger than the similarities. The basic differences between the two thinkers may be illustrated in Marx's own terms: Marx's analysis focused on the "foundation" of bourgeois society, the capitalistic economic system or mode of production, whereas Tocqueville's focus was the "superstructure," the social psychology of men in middle-class society. Finally, of course, the most obvious and fundamental difference was that for Tocqueville bourgeois society was basically and increasingly equalitarian, while for Marx it was a society characterized by its own distinctive classes and class antagonisms. So although Tocqueville's analysis yields definite insights, the fact that he slighted the "foundation" caused him, as we shall later see, to miss some of the most significant structural trends of American society at the time.

DEMOCRATIC MIDDLE-CLASS SOCIETY

In democratic societies, scientific, industrial, and commercial values are paramount, and education is largely centered on these values. What do democratic nations love? "Physical gratification," the idea of improving one's condition, competition, success — it is these that become the main motives of men. Tocqueville recognized how "all men who live in democratic times more or less contract the ways of thinking of the manufacturing and trading classes. . . ." [1] This is true of all democracies but "applicable in its full extent only to America . . ." (208).

Democratic societies are tumultuous and restless, as compared with aristocratic societies; and men seek productivity even in their pleasures: "they want to mix actual fruition with their joy," and "they prefer those more serious and silent amusements which are like business and which do not drive business wholly out of their minds" (221). All their thoughts are turned toward the acquisition of private fortune, and it is primarily this motive that accounts for their ceaseless, restless activity. Democracy in these terms, Tocqueville sensed, is a modern phenomenon and has nothing in common with what was called "democracy" among the ancients.

Throughout, Tocqueville is acutely aware that a new social order has

---

[1] Alexis de Tocqueville, *Democracy in America*, the Henry Reeve text, revised by Frances Bowen, and further corrected and edited with an introduction, editorial notes, and bibliographies, by Phillip Bradley (New York: Knopf, 1948). Page references to Volume II of this work will hereafter appear in parentheses immediately following the quoted passage.

come into being that contrasts sharply with the old, which he calls aristocracy. New social and political conditions have transformed man's character. A new type of man has emerged. In democracies, men never stand still and are always animated. They have many passions and motives but these end in or proceed from a "love of riches." Money becomes more important than ever before; money has become an end, so that the cooperation of men may not be obtained without paying for it. All other distinctions vanish before money, which becomes the sole means by which men hope to raise themselves above their fellows. The love of wealth drives men into "business and manufacture," particularly in America where other opportunities to enrich oneself, as by war or public office, are minimal (229). A leveling, a sameness, results; men increasingly think, feel, and act alike.

The very notion of honor has been basically transformed. In America, that bourgeois civilization par excellence, the quiet virtues that tend to encourage business are held in honor. Men are "constantly driven to engage in commerce and industry. Their origin, their social condition, and even the region they inhabit urge them irresistibly in this direction" (235). America is a manufacturing and commercial civilization "placed in the midst of a new and boundless country, which their principal object is to explore for purposes of profit" (235). Manners, morals, and virtues are evaluated as they affect success in business. One sees a type of courage here but not the courage of the old, European feudal order. In America, courage is rather that which "emboldens men to brave the dangers of the ocean in order to arrive earlier in port . . ." (237). Idleness, held in such high esteem by the leisure class of the old order, is the most contemptible trait in the new — where work is honorable, that is, work in the professions, in commerce, and in industry.

In democracies, man is as dynamic as the ever-changing conditions of his life. In the Middle Ages, in contrast, man was "ever stationary," "and the state of opinions was hardly more changeable than that of conditions" (238). Tocqueville understood in general that the class structure of a society shapes and directs men's conduct; that manners, morals, virtue, and honor vary with class position. Because for Tocqueville the great middle class in America dominated everything, there was, correspondingly, great cultural conformity. In a democracy like France, on the other hand, where classes prevailed, including vestigial elements of the old order, there were also "conflicting notions of honor" (239).

Where, as in America, men ceaselessly pursue property, power, and reputation, where hardly anyone is destitute of property or knowledge, and where no class barriers exist, ambition is universal. But it is not a "lofty ambition," because all their human faculties are used "to achieve paltry results, and this cannot fail speedily to limit their range of view and to circumscribe their powers" (245). Moreover, even in an open, democratic society, where formal legal barriers do not prevent men from rising or advancing, "competition attains the same end." "In a well established democratic community," Tocqueville writes, "great and rapid elevation is therefore rare; it forms an exception to the common rule; and it is the singularity of such occurrences that makes men forget how rarely they happen" (246). Thus Tocqueville underscores, from his aristocratic standpoint, the mediocrity and meanness of men's values, activities, ambitions, and achievements in the new society.

INDUSTRY, COMMERCE, AND LOVE OF WELL-BEING

In democratic society men are diverted from agriculture and develop a taste for commerce and industry. But if commerce and manufacturing enhance the "taste for physical well-being" they do not cause it. If one must speak in terms of cause and effect, Tocqueville maintained, then it is equality that engenders a taste for well-being which, in turn, encourages trade and industry. America seemed to validate this hypothesis, because in that society in which traditional barriers had never existed, industrial progress was without parallel. No "people in the world have made such rapid progress in trade and manufactures as the Americans" (156). At the same time, he saw the beginnings of what Marx later described as the economic crises of capitalism. However, their respective interpretations of the phenomenon of crisis differ fundamentally. Marx sought its cause in the inherent workings of the modern economic system; in this sense his explanation was structural. Tocqueville, in contrast, attributed the ultimate cause of the "endemic disease" to the social psychology of democratic nations:

As they [the Americans] are all engaged in commerce, their commercial affairs are affected by such various and complex causes that it is impossible to foresee what difficulties may arise. As they are all more or less engaged in productive industry, at the least shock given to business all private fortunes are put in jeopardy at the same time, and the state is shaken. I believe that the return of these commercial panics is an endemic disease of the democratic nations of our age. It may be rendered less dangerous, but it cannot be cured, because it does not originate in accidental circumstances, *but in the temperament of these nations* (italics added, 157).

Land and agriculture were also increasingly commercialized. Not only do men produce for the market, they bring "land into tillage" not to farm it but to sell it. They build "a farmhouse on the speculation that, as the state of the country will soon be changed by the increase of population, a good price may be obtained for it" (157). Tocqueville overwhelmingly emphasized the commercial materialistic character and psychology of men in democratic societies. All pursuits of men are dominated by bourgeois commercial values.

Yet, however prosperous men may be in democratic society, they are forever restless and never satisfied. Craving always more of whatever they have, men are always serious, almost sad. They are "forever brooding over advantages they do not possess" (136). It is in the nature of such a society that men cling to worldly goods and pursue more and more of them as if they fear dying before they can enjoy them. Tocqueville thus drew attention to a supreme restlessness in the midst of abundance as well as a fetishism of material goods. And ultimately his master concept, "equality," accounts for these conditions. He used equality to refer to those social relations in which men are no longer severely separated from one another by caste and class barriers. Therefore each social difference appears larger and "the desire of equality always becomes more insatiable in proportion as equality is more complete" (138). Like Émile Durkheim after him, Tocqueville suggests that these insatiable appetites affect modern man in the depth of his soul and result in suicide, mental disorders, and other "symptoms of the same disease" (139). Tocqueville's phrase, "taste for physical well-being," was therefore partially ironic; for this taste led, in his view, neither to a real well-being nor to a sense of it.

What caused him concern was not any alleged "sumptuous depravity" of democratic peoples, which, after all, was more characteristic of aristocracies. Rather, it was that in a democracy men dwell upon small objects by which they are absorbed and to which their souls cling. The danger he saw was that a "virtuous materialism may ultimately be established in the world, which would not corrupt, but enervate the soul and noiselessly unbend its springs of action" (133).

CLASSES IN THE OLD ORDER

Equalitarian democracies, in all their aspects, could best be understood if one contrasted them with the old order, based on social classes. In an aristocracy, there is great esprit de corps among the members of each class, produced by the great commonality of conditions, the common fate, that the members of each class share. The relatively closed character of the classes enhances the degree to which the members of each class feel a strong human sympathy for one another but not for the members of other classes. Great differences exist among the separate classes in the thoughts, feelings, rights, duties, and way of life of their respective members. It is as if the separate classes were separate races or species, for in effect they do not and, typically, perhaps cannot relate to each other primarily as human beings.

The ties between noble and serf, for example, are not first of all human ties. The great social and cultural chasm lying between them makes it virtually impossible that the noble should have any human feelings toward the serf. The ties between them are strictly socio-political — of lord to vassal — and not of man to man. The chroniclers of the Middle Ages show great grief for the dead noble but "tell you . . . without wincing of massacres and tortures inflicted on the common sort of people." Because the nobles "had formed no clear notion of a poor man's suffering, they cared but little for his fate" (163), which, in turn, resulted in "atrocious barbarities practiced from time to time by the lower classes on the higher" (164). Tocqueville relates that in 1675 a revolt of the lower classes, at the imposition of a new tax, was suppressed with great cruelty. He cites the correspondence of Madame de Sévigné to illustrate the effects of class barriers on human sensitivity. In this respect typical of the other members of her class, she remained unmoved at the suffering of those who were not persons of "quality."

With equality, however, all this is significantly changed, because all men now think and feel more nearly alike. They more easily enter into one another's feelings, and their common humanity is more obvious. Americans, by achieving an outstanding degree of equality, are therefore also a very compassionate people. What applies to individuals within a nation applies to nations as well: great social and cultural differences among them cause a frame of mind that Tocqueville illustrates with the writings of Cicero, for whom "a barbarian did not belong to the same human race as a Roman" (167).

In the old order rank was acquired by birth; definite and fixed social barriers separated noble from commoner. Social intercourse between them, which was always quite limited and never on an equal footing, never engendered in the upper classes a fear of losing status by associating with the lower. However, as a "moneyed aristocracy" developed, privileges, although remaining great, no longer exclusively belonged to the aristocracy of birth. The privileged now become fearful of losing or sharing their advantageous positions and they struggle with those who want either to usurp or to share those positions. Typically, then, although an individual "seeks to raise himself into a higher circle, he is always on the defensive against the intrusion of those below him" (169). In equalitarian America, finally, social intercourse for the greatest number is natural, frank, free, and open, and neither constrained nor restricted by considerations of class and status. For Tocqueville, classless America had already largely traversed the general historical path that European societies were destined to follow. The concept of class, therefore, would soon lose its utility. A concept valuable for analyzing the old, predemocratic order will be useless for analyzing the new. But he was not altogether sure.

CLASSES IN A DEMOCRACY?
Tocqueville did in fact perceive certain class divisions in the democracy, i.e., between those who owned property and those who owned little or none and labored for the former. These divisions were temporary, however, and destined to disappear with the inexorable growth of equality. Generally, when he spoke of workers, he did not distinguish between those of agriculture and those of industry. When he wrote, therefore, that it appears to be a great social law that wages will rise in proportion to the general equality of conditions, he considered mainly the "wages" of agricultural laborers who

> are themselves owners of certain plots of ground, which just enable them to subsist without working for anyone else. When these laborers come to offer their services to a neighboring landowner or farmer, if he refuses them a certain rate of wages they retire to their own small property and await another opportunity (189–190).

When, however, Tocqueville turned from agriculture to manufacturing industry, he saw "a great and gloomy exception" to his general social law. He drew the reader's attention to the fact that a new "aristocracy" has emerged in "productive industry and has established its sway there . . ." (190). The fact that he calls it an "aristocracy" is perhaps indicative, for although he described rather well the social consequences of its sway, he did not appreciate that this industrial aristocracy was the beginning of a new socio-economic system (which Marx later called "capitalism") that will increasingly become dominant.

Tocqueville discerned in democratic society an emerging social relationship, comparable to that between master and slave. In the new form of servitude the workers are "almost at the mercy of the master." They "soon contract habits of body and mind which unfit them for any other toil." The masters can combine and reduce wages; and if and when the workers strike:

> The master, who is a rich man, can very well wait, without being ruined, until necessity brings them back to him; but they [the workers] must work day by day or they die, for their only property is in their hands. They have long been impoverished by oppression, and the poorer they become, the more easily they may be oppressed; they can never escape from this fatal circle of cause and consequence (190).

Thus Tocqueville observed a new form of dependence, accompanied by great human wretchedness, emerging among the manufacturing populations of all modern democracies, including the United States. And if it appeared "exceptional," it was no less ominous on that account. ". . . [W]hen the whole of a society is in motion," wrote Tocqueville in a proposition that seems equally valid today, "it is difficult to keep any one class stationary, and when the greater number of men are opening new paths to fortune, it is no less difficult to make the few support in peace their wants and their desires" (191).

In democracies, labor had a certain evident dignity; in America, outside the slave states, this was especially true. In this middle-class country, par excellence, industrial and commercial occupations were held in high esteem; "every honest calling is honorable." This esteem was so great that, Tocqueville noted, when rich Americans wanted to escape the duty to work they went to Europe where the remnants of aristocratic society still held idleness in honor and despised labor — especially labor for profit. In democracies, not merely labor but labor joined to the profit motive was regarded as both necessary and honorable — again this was presumably more characteristic of America than the other democracies that retained aristocratic elements. Nevertheless, it did not escape Tocqueville that in democratic society one could observe not only invidious distinctions among types of work and labor, but even a dichotomy between independent work and dependent labor.

In his discussion of the aristocracy of manufactures, Tocqueville describes the two main classes of the industrial system. Although he only indirectly alludes to Adam Smith's treatment of the division of labor in manufacturing, Tocqueville acknowledges, as later did Marx, the validity of much that Smith and the other classical economists had to say. Like Marx, Tocqueville saw the various technical advantages of the modern division of labor: commodities are "produced with greater ease, speed, and economy"; and the costs of production are lowered as the amount of capital and the scale of production grow larger. But it was as evident to Tocqueville as to Marx that the flesh-and-blood worker paid a great price for the gains in productivity: the worker was to that extent diminished as a human being.

Tocqueville grasped much of what Marx later described as *alienation,* the process over which the worker had no control and by which he was divested of all his human faculties, and even the need for those faculties; the process by which he became poorer as a human being the more he produced, since his best energy was consumed and reified in commodities; the process, finally, by which he was chained to one debilitating position in the division of labor. What happens to a man when he becomes a detail laborer? Tocqueville's reply could easily be fitted into the appropriate sections of Marx's early essays on alienated labor as well as his later treatment of the same phenomenon in *Capital,* so compatible is it with his conception. Tocqueville wrote:

> When a workman is unceasingly and exclusively engaged in the fabrication of one thing, he ultimately does his work with singular dexterity; but at the same time he loses the general faculty of applying his mind to the direction of the work. He every day becomes more adroit and less industrious; so that it may be said that in proportion as the workman improves, the man is degraded. What can be expected of a man who has spent twenty years of his life in making heads for pins? (158)

> When a workman has spent a considerable portion of his existence in this manner, his thoughts are forever set upon the object of his daily toil; his body has contracted certain fixed habits, which it can never shake off; in a word, he no longer belongs to himself, but to the calling that he has chosen. It is in vain that laws and manners have been at pains to level all the barriers round such a man and to open to him on every side a thousand different paths to fortune; a theory of manufactures more powerful than customs and laws binds him to a craft, and frequently to a spot, which he cannot leave; it assigns to him a certain place in society, beyond which he cannot go; in the midst of universal movement it has rendered him stationary (158–159).

Marx later also described the dehumanizing consequences of the modern division of labor. Its higher productivity was made possible precisely by dividing, classifying, and grouping the workers according to narrow and specific functions. What was taken away from the individual worker in artistic skill, creativity, and reflective powers, in the need for knowledge, judgment, and will, was imparted to the organization. The deficiencies of the former became the virtues of the latter. The whole organization was enriched by alienating the worker from his individual powers.

Tocqueville viewed the consequences of the manufacturing process similarly:

> In proportion as the principle of the division of labor is more extensively applied, the workman becomes more weak, more narrow-minded, and more dependent. The art advances, the artisan recedes. On the other hand, in proportion as it becomes more manifest that the productions of manufactures are by so much the cheaper and better as the manufacture is larger and the amount of capital employed more considerable, wealthy and educated men come forward to embark in manufactures, which were heretofore abandoned to poor or ignorant handicraftsmen. The magnitude of the efforts required and the importance of the results to be obtained attract them. Thus at the very time at which the science of manufactures lowers the class of workmen, it raises the class of masters (159).

And further describing the emerging social dichotomy, accompanying the new productive system, he continues:

> While the workman concentrates his faculties more and more upon the study of a single detail, the master surveys an extensive whole, and the mind of the latter is enlarged in proportion as that of the former is narrowed. In a short time the one will require nothing but physical strength without intelligence; the other stands in need of science, and almost of genius, to ensure success. This man resembles more and more the administrator of a vast empire; that man, a brute.
>
> The master and the workman have then here no similarity, and their differences increase every day. They are connected only like the two rings at the extremities of a long chain. Each of them fills the station which is made for him, and which he does not leave; the one is continually, closely, and necessarily dependent upon the other and seems as much born to obey as that other is to command. What is this but aristocracy? (159)

Yet it would be quite erroneous to infer from this that Tocqueville had anticipated Marx's theory. It is true that Tocqueville perceived the two main classes of the new economic system, the process by which one class was able to exploit and oppress the other and their conflicting interests and contrasting conditions. He also recognized that the social relations between master and worker were strictly instrumental: "The manufacturer asks nothing of the workman but his labor; the workman expects nothing from him but his wages" (160). On balance, however, although he saw the harshness of the new aristocracy, "one of the harshest that ever existed in the world," he also felt it was "one of the most confined and least dangerous." Tocqueville had already seen the most advanced capitalist industry of his time, in Manchester, England; he also had visited the industrial cities of the United States. Yet he continued to regard manufacturing industry as an "exceptional" phenomenon and did not appreciate that the new mode of production would progressively supersede the old and become the rule. Tocqueville recognized the growth and potential dominance of capitalist industry only as a remote possibility. He urged those who cherished democracy to keep their eyes fixed on the manufacturing aristocracy "for *if* ever a permanent inequality of conditions and aristocracy again penetrates into the world, it may be predicted that this is the gate by which they will enter" (161, italics added). Tocqueville's attitude toward industry will be taken up again later in our critical observations and in connection with his visits to England.

REVOLUTION IN DEMOCRATIC SOCIETY
The concept of class was among the most important in Tocqueville's analysis of the structure of society and the historical changes it had undergone. This is evident throughout his work, but particularly in his analysis of the conditions conducing to revolution. He used class relations to explain the more or less violent form social change assumed in different societies. Indeed, among his main purposes in studying America and England was to understand why the movement toward democracy and equality appeared less violent and more peaceful in those countries than in his own. His studies of all three countries seemed to yield the following generalization (which also seemed to explain what had become so evident about the democratic movement in France):

> A people that has existed for centuries under a system of castes and classes can arrive at a democratic state of society only by passing through a long series of more or less critical transformations, accomplished by violent efforts, and after numerous vicissitudes, in the course of which property, opinions, and power are rapidly transferred from one to another (251).

As these revolutionary upheavals appear to occur precisely while equality is becoming greater, not diminishing, many see a causal link between the two. But is it equality that leads to revolution? "I do not believe it,"

40

says Tocqueville. He categorically rejects the presumed causal link between growing equality and violent revolution.

The great revolutions of the past had been caused by *inequality;* and with the growth of equality "great revolutions will become more rare." "Almost all the revolutions that have changed the aspect of nations have been made to consolidate or to destroy social inequality" (252). The society, then, in which one might least expect revolutionary upheavals is one "in which every man shall have something to keep and little to take from others . . ." (252).

In aristocratic society, the great masses of the people are poor while the very rich are few. An aristocratic society is sharply divided between a very small but rich minority and a very large but poor majority with intermediate strata virtually nonexistent. The majority, moreover, is irrevocably bound to its position. In a democracy there are also rich and poor. However, in this case, in contrast with the aristocracy, the extremes are numerically small and neither position is permanent, as neither is guaranteed by laws of heredity. Finally and most important, unlike aristocracies, where intermediate strata hardly exist, democracies are based on a large middle class:

> an innumerable multitude of men almost alike, who, without being exactly either rich or poor, possess sufficient property to desire the maintenance of order, yet not enough to excite envy. Such men are the natural enemies of violent commotions; their lack of agitation keeps all beneath them and above them still and secures the balance of the fabric of society (252).

In this society the moderate fortunes of the overwhelming majority conduce to moderate politics and social order. Ultimately, small property is the mainstay of this order. Moreover, in democracies it is not only the possession of property but the great importance that the large class of small property holders attribute to their "scanty fortunes" that minimizes the likelihood of revolution. Most men believe that they have something to lose and little or nothing to gain from a revolutionary upheaval. For all these reasons growing equality suggests to Tocqueville that great revolutions would become rarer — all the more so in America where the victory of equality and property appeared definitive. But the possibility of revolution by minorities still remained, as Tocqueville wrote: "If ever America undergoes great revolutions, they will be brought about by the presence of the black race on the soil of the United States; that is to say, they will owe their origin, not to the equality, but to the inequality of condition" (256). Democracies, therefore, are vulnerable to revolution as a consequence of whatever inequalities prevail. "In democratic communities," Tocqueville wrote, "revolutions are seldom desired except by a minority, but a minority may sometimes effect them" (256).

SOCIOLOGY OF KNOWLEDGE, CULTURE, AND RELIGION

Tocqueville was among those modern thinkers, including Marx, who, following Montesquieu, attempted to understand why men thought and believed as they did by relating their ideas to their existential conditions. As applied to America, this principle suggested that if the American philosophical method or consciousness was eminently secular, democratic, practical, and experimental, these characteristics reflected the general social conditions in that nation.

The American consciousness was democratic, that is, peculiar to the middle classes; it was democratic and equalitarian in that it was believed that ". . . the greater truth should go with the greater number" (10). Correspondingly, great faith existed in public opinion. Actually, the American philosophical method revealed two tendencies. On the one hand, Americans were inclined to try the untried; they were practical and experimental and rose to the challenge of a recalcitrant environment. But on the other hand, they apparently conformed mindlessly with the opinions of the majority.

Tocqueville's sociological conception of knowledge led him to see rather clearly how inequality and equality affect the beliefs men hold. Where inequalities are great and of long duration, the men of different social classes tend to regard one another as if they were members of distinct races. Inequality, therefore, militates against a general view. Under democracy and equality, in contrast, men tend to see their common humanity. Equality also leads Everyman to investigate the truth for himself because he has no class of intellectual superiors to set an example or show him the way. He has great curiosity but little leisure; his life is practical, confused, excited, and active, and he craves easy success and present enjoyment. If he has a predilection for general ideas and little patience for detail, it is mainly in those areas in which he is not directly and practically occupied every day.

The Americans are a practical people and their pragmatic, empirical attitude, itself a product of American social conditions, inclines them less to theory and more to practice, which applies also to science. Americans mistrust abstract systems and "visionary speculation." They do not easily defer to authority, precedent, or "schools"; they prefer plain English to "big words," and "they adhere closely to facts and study facts with their own senses" (41). Not that they altogether ignore theory in science; far from it. They pay the most careful attention "to the theoretical portion which is immediately requisite to application" (42).

The main reason for the pronounced practicality of American science and knowledge may be found in the American way of life and the structure of American society. The restlessness, the unceasing quest for gain, for power, and for fortune, tend to preclude the calm and leisure so necessary for meditation. And nothing, perhaps, is so important for the higher sciences than meditation. In America — and to a lesser extent in other democratic societies — agitation is constant, an "incessant jostling of men, which annoys and disturbs the mind without exciting or elevating it" (43). Therefore a definite anti-intellectualism exists in America — mainly because there has not been a leading and honorific intellectual stratum in that country. Men rarely meditate and have little esteem for those who do. The American is a man of action, so although he is interested in the truth and accuracy of his ideas, he prefers to act, using information at hand, rather than to research every idea to the bottom. He believes that "in the long run he risks less in making use of some false principles than in spending his time in establishing all his principles on the basis of truth" (43).

Tocqueville linked this attitude to the love of physical well-being. To men living in the democratic age "every new method that leads by a shorter road to wealth, every machine that spares labor, every instrument that diminishes the cost of production, every discovery that facilitates pleasures or augments them, seems to be the grandest effort of the human intellect" (45). In democracies, these materialistic motives guide and shape science; material interest draws the mind away from the "loftier spheres — down to the middle zone," for science is eminently practical and applied. In aristocracies, in contrast, science is cultivated for its own sake and highly theoretical but often confined "to the arrogant and sterile research for abstract truths . . ." (46).

Aristocracies stress the beautiful, and quality is the highest virtue of the product of manufacture. That which was not a consideration at all in aristocracies — namely, manufacturing with the greatest speed and the lowest cost — attains utmost importance in democracies. In the aristocracy, the customers are the aristocratic few and the craftsman relies on the perfection of his workmanship to appeal to their loftier tastes. Even the peasant would "rather go without the objects he covets than procure them in a state of imperfection" (49). In democracies, on the other hand, the middle- and lower-class customers, the great multitude, cannot afford real objets d'art and would rather have a poor imitation or imperfect object than none at all. Correspondingly, the manufacturer seeks to make as many such items as possible, at the least cost. Hence, a middling standard, mediocrity, becomes the rule in all the arts.

Although Tocqueville's discussion of the "mass" or "popular" culture of democracies may be construed as criticizing this tendency from an aristocratic standpoint, it should not be supposed that he was uncritical of art and literature dominated by aristocratic values. Because, in aristocracies, the members of the literary class often live among themselves and speak and write for themselves and the very few, their art is often infected with a "false and labored style." In their effort to keep themselves separate from the lower classes, they develop "a sort of aristocratic jargon which is hardly less remote from pure language than is the coarse dialect of the people. Such are the natural perils of literature among aristocracies. Every aristocracy that keeps itself aloof from the people becomes impotent, a fact which is as true in literature as it is in politics" (58).

Literature and art, then, are profoundly influenced by the social and political condition of a nation. "Democracy," writes Tocqueville, "not only infuses a taste for letters among the trading classes, but introduces a trading spirit into literature." And again: "Democratic literature is always infested with a tribe of writers who look upon letters as a mere trade; and for the same few great authors who adorn it, you may reckon thousands of idea-mongers" (61).

The general thesis — that bourgeois huckstering values increasingly dominate and permeate the activities and thoughts of democratic man — applies also to language: not only does the general agitation tend to change the character of the language, but many new words appear, borrowed mostly from industry and trade. The "majority lays down the law in language as well as in everything else," and because the majority is engaged in business and industry, its language bears the mark of these occupations. The general tendency of democracies to lower class barriers also results in lowering linguistic barriers so that "all the words of a language are mingled" (68). The common store of words increases, and mutually unintelligible dialects disappear.

Similarly, the character of historiography and social science is transformed in the transition from aristocratic to democratic society. The aristocratic historian tends to see a few prominent actors, a few great men, who occupy the entire historical stage and who allegedly make history; the democratic historian sees large social forces and general causes — corresponding to the new situation in which the people have a greater role to play. There was, however, a dangerous tendency among the historians of the democratic age: they tend to divorce actions from the actors; they reify actions and organize them into sequences and systems. In this way they not only deny the influence on history of the few; they even "deprive the people themselves of the power of modifying their own condition, and they subject them either to an inflexible providence or to some blind necessity" (87).

RELIGION AND COMMERCE

Religion could also be analyzed in relation to social conditions. Where social stratification is minimal and equality greatest, men are inclined to "conceive of the idea of the one God . . . ; while on the contrary in a state of society where men are broken up into very unequal ranks, they are apt to devise as many deities as there are· nations, castes, [and] classes . . ." (23).

The appeal of Christian teachings to the early Christians may be understood by seeing that they were all equal in their oppressed status under the Caesars. With the dissolution later of the Roman empire and the growth of feudalism, the proliferation of saints may be viewed as a consequence of the "distribution of mankind into fractions. . . . Unable to subdivide the Deity . . . [men] multiplied and unduly enhanced the importance of his agents" (24). Still later, with the ascendancy of democracy and equality, the more social barriers were removed or lowered, the more men moved "towards the idea of a single and all-powerful being . . ." (24).

Tocqueville perceived the connection between religion and worldly interests: "Americans follow their religion from interest." American preachers were always "referring to the earth, and it is only with great difficulty that they can divert their attention from it" (127). And, describing their discourses, Tocqueville continues: ". . . it is often difficult to ascertain . . . whether the principal object of religion is to procure eternal felicity in the other world or prosperity in this" (127). America, for Tocqueville, was uniquely bourgeois: "Not only are manufacturing and commercial classes to be found in the United States, as they are in all countries, but, what never occurred elsewhere, the whole community is simultaneously engaged in productive industry and commerce" (35–36). He noted the exceptional position of the Americans in this respect as well as the preponderantly Puritanical background of the independent merchants and entrepreneurs. The values of Puritanism on the one hand

45

and of commerce and industry on the other appeared not only compatible but mutually reinforcing. Although Tocqueville includes other elements that apparently contributed to the peculiarly practical temperament of the Americans, he mentions first their "strictly Puritanical origin [and] their exclusively commercial habits . . ." (36–37). These people spent "every day in the week in making money, and Sunday in going to Church . . ." (83). Apparently, this was so characteristic, particularly in New England, that Thomas Hamilton described it in much the same way. And neither Hamilton's nor Tocqueville's descriptions later escaped the attention of the young Marx when he wanted to illustrate the effective domination of a society by the huckstering mentality.[2]

BUREAUCRACY IN DEMOCRATIC SOCIETY

For Tocqueville, a large, centralized state bureaucracy was perhaps the greatest hazard to liberty — all the more so when, as in France, the older forms of local and provincial autonomy had been fatally weakened or destroyed without being replaced by new forms. Add to this the bureaucratic careerism and place-hunting that accompanied the growth of the centralized administration, and one sees how bureaucracy could become an immense and effective instrument of despotism. It centralized power and at the same time destroyed the spirit of independence by infecting a large section of the populace with a "venal and servile attitude." Throughout continental Europe, Tocqueville observed, "the government rules in two ways: it rules one portion of the citizens by the fear which they feel for its agents, and the other by the hope they have of becoming its agents" (305n). This was conspicuously absent from America, where men sought their fortunes by their own efforts in commerce, industry, and agriculture.

Like Marx, Tocqueville viewed the development of a centralized state bureaucracy as a function of class conflict: the bureaucracy was, among other things, an instrument of classes in the conflict among them. Where the struggle of the middle and lower classes with the old order was long and arduous, as it had been in France, the supreme power was concentrated and strong. Both the revolution and the counter-revolution contributed to this.

If in America, in contrast, no such supreme centralized power existed, it was because: "The inhabitants of the United States were never divided

---

[2] See Karl Marx, *Early Writings*, translated and edited by T. B. Bottomore, (London: C. A. Watts & Co. Ltd.), pp. 35ff.

by any privileges; they have never known the mutual relation of master and inferior; and as they neither dread nor hate each other, they have never known the necessity of calling in the supreme power to manage their affairs." The Americans are singular in this regard "because they have no aristocracy to combat" (299). But England, too, was singular. She had preserved her aristocracy together with its high regard for private rights and local liberty — and had avoided extreme administrative centralization besides. Therefore one had to learn from the English as well as the American experience for both nations had so far escaped France's fate.

3. Critical Observations

ONE OF THE EARLIEST American critics of *Democracy in America* was Jared Sparks, whom Tocqueville had first met in Paris in 1828 while the former was searching in the French archives for materials on American history. Three years later, when Tocqueville came to America and had some difficulties comprehending the process of town government in New England, he enlisted Sparks' assistance. Expressly at Tocqueville's and Beaumont's request, Sparks wrote a special memoir, "Observations on the Town Governments of Massachusetts," which became one of Tocqueville's most important sources of information.[1]

The two men became rather good friends. Sparks assisted Tocqueville in many ways which included arranging the publication of his report on the emancipation of slaves in the French colonies (published in the *North American Review,* circa July 1840). And Tocqueville reciprocated by helping Sparks obtain original French materials on American history. Sparks' edition of *Life and Correspondence of Gouverneur Morris* was also translated and published in France through Tocqueville's influence.

Nevertheless, despite their friendship, mutual respect, and assistance, Sparks did not hesitate to level against Tocqueville's work several telling criticisms. For example, in a letter dated February 1, 1841, to Major Poussin of Paris, who had written a book on American government and institutions, Sparks criticized Tocqueville for occasionally allowing his theories to lead him astray, especially his theory on the "tyranny of

---

[1] See *Jared Sparks and Alexis de Tocqueville,* ed., Herbert B. Adams in Johns Hopkins University Studies in Historical and Political Science, vol. XVI, no. 12 (Baltimore: Johns Hopkins University Press, 1898), pp. 7–49.

the majority." Indeed, Sparks believed, Tocqueville was "entirely mistaken. His ideas are not verified by experience." Sparks argued that if such a tyranny existed, it would have to be in the making of the laws; therefore any evil arising out of such laws would have to have precisely the same effect upon the majority as upon the minority.[2] Furthermore, a majority that passed oppressive laws would "certainly be changed at the next election, and be composed of different elements. M. de Tocqueville's theory can only be true where the majority is an unchangeable body and where it acts exclusively on the minority, as distinct from itself, — a state of things which can never occur where the elections are frequent and every man has a voice in choosing the legislators." [3]

In another letter dated October 13, 1841, to Professor William Smyth of Cambridge, England, Sparks criticized Smyth's lectures on America, which were apparently based on Tocqueville's theory of the tyranny of the majority. In this letter Sparks makes points very similar to those he made earlier and observed, in addition, that ". . . M. de Tocqueville often confounds the majority with public opinion, which has the same tendency, or nearly so, in all civilized countries, whatever may be the form of government." [4]

In a later letter, dated June 13, 1853, to Tocqueville, Sparks called attention, among other things, to the immense material progress taking place in the United States at the time, a development which Tocqueville, under the influence of his predominantly agrarian model of America, had shown no real signs of anticipating. "The rapid growth of cities, towns, and villages," wrote Sparks, "the expansion of commerce, the increasing products of agriculture, the multiplication of railroads forming a network from the eastern extremity of Maine to the Mississippi, and of steamboats floating on all navigable rivers and lakes, the *vast increase of manufactures of every description* — all these present a scene of rapid change, activity, enterprise and progress which certainly has no parallel in the history of civilization." [5]

Sparks shifts in the next sentence of the letter to culture and education. Although he seems to have been acknowledging to Tocqueville that it would be a long time "before there will be a large class who will seek eminence by triumphs in literature or purely intellectual achievements," he also insists, in opposition to Tocqueville's view, that

---

[2] *Ibid.,* pp. 43–44.

[3] *Ibid.*

[4] *Ibid.*

[5] *Ibid.,* p. 45. Italics added.

American democracy was already then making it evident that its mass culture did not preclude the rather impressive development of institutions of higher learning and higher culture. Indeed, as several of Tocqueville's critics were later to point out, some of the world's most outstanding writers emerged in America almost as soon as he had virtually denied such a possibility.

Among these critics was James Bryce, the author of the later classic account of American society and institutions. Although Bryce highly respected Tocqueville's work, he deemed it necessary in his famous essay, "The Predictions of Hamilton and Tocqueville," to call attention to several important developments that Tocqueville failed either to observe or "to appraise at their due value." [6] Bryce criticized Tocqueville for missing the significance of the party organization system, the spoils system, and the growth of commerce, particularly the latter's contribution to the increasing interdependence of the separate states and to the substantial decline in the "power of state sentiment." In addition, Bryce noted that Tocqueville had missed the abolitionist movement. The abolitionists had begun to organize themselves before he arrived in the United States and had formed the National Anti-Slavery Society in 1833; yet, Tocqueville noted neither the movement nor the hostility it aroused in the South.

Like Sparks, Bryce also suggested that at times Tocqueville's mass-culture thesis assumed the character of a dogma, blinding him to the possibility of higher cultural achievements in America, to the "growth of the literary spirit and the beginnings of literary production." Although Tocqueville had visited Boston, he never mentioned the society with which one associates such names as Hawthorne, Emerson, Longfellow, Channing, Thoreau, Prescott, Ticknor, Fuller, and others.[7]

Bryce was also among the first to suggest that Tocqueville's equalitarian model of American society obscured money's increasing influence on politics. As Bryce wrote:

It might have been foretold that in a country with such resources and among a people of such restless commercial activity, great piles of wealth

---

[6] James Bryce, *The Predictions of Hamilton and Tocqueville* in Johns Hopkins University Studies in Historical and Political Science, vol. 5, Herbert B. Adams, Editor (Baltimore: Publications Agency of the Johns Hopkins University, 1887), p. 49.

[7] *Ibid.*, p. 48.

would soon be accumulated, that this wealth would find objects which it might accomplish by legislative aid, would seek to influence government, and would find ample opportunity for doing so. But of the dangers that must thence arise we do not hear a word.[8]

In short, although Tocqueville characteristically preoccupied himself with his fears of the "majority" and the "masses," the dangers to democracy that accompanied the concentration of wealth went unnoticed.

Tocqueville never foresaw the stupendous "growth of great fortunes, and of wealthy and powerful trading corporations. . . ." Nor did he foresee such accompanying political developments as the "Perfection and hierarchical consolidation, of nominally representative, but really oligarchic lines, of party organization, and the consequent growth of Rings and Bosses, and demoralization of city government." [9] Tocqueville not only failed to foresee the most characteristic inequalities of the near future; he also missed those that prevailed during his visit, inequalities that other contemporary visitors to America noted well. It might therefore be instructive to compare Tocqueville's observations with those of another famous Frenchman, Michel Chevalier, who traveled in the United States at about the same time (from 1833 to 1835).

TOCQUEVILLE'S BLINDNESS TO THE GROWTH OF CAPITALISM

Chevalier had also come to the United States in behalf of the French government, but to study the canal and railroad systems; like Tocqueville he exploited the opportunity to study many other aspects of American social life. His observations were first published in France in 1836 as *Lettres sur l'Amérique du Nord*. Three years later they were translated and published in Boston as *Society, Manners, and Politics in the United States; Being a Series of Letters on North America*.[10] In contrast with Tocqueville's highly abstract and philosophical treatment of American conditions and institutions, Chevalier's is most often concretely descriptive and empirical. More important, however, is the significantly different standpoint from which he viewed America. Chevalier was a Saint-Simonian and as such bound to concern himself with science, industry, the economic system, and social power. As a result, one learns many things from Chevalier that one could never learn from Tocqueville.

---

[8] *Ibid.*, p. 49.
[9] *Ibid.*, pp. 50–51.
[10] John W. Ward, ed., (Garden City, N.Y.: Doubleday Anchor, 1961).

Chevalier recognized, for example, that the economy was already expanding phenomenally and transforming the United States from an agrarian into a commercial-industrial society. The Americans were speculating in cotton, land, city and town lots (real estate), banks, and railroads. In the North they vied with one another for valuable timberlands; in the South for cotton lands. While Tocqueville never described a single town or city in the United States and certainly never attributed to the city any long-range social or historical significance, Chevalier centered attention on the increasing urbanization, commercialization, and industrialization of the society. He noted that although Chicago at the time had only two or three thousand inhabitants, the land for some twenty-five miles around had been sold — enough land to accommodate 300,000 inhabitants, or "more than any city of the New World presently contains." [11] Chevalier also understood that the enormous railroad expansion meant that this mode of transportation was destined to supersede the older ones.

Although Chevalier, like Tocqueville, was impressed with the democratic-equalitarian atmosphere in the United States, he also noted the specific impact democratic values had upon the workers. He called attention to the prevailing social inequalities and their consequences, particularly to the working class and its unrest. Chevalier provided at least a glimpse of the classes, class consciousness, and class conflicts of Jacksonian America — something, again, one could never learn from *Democracy in America*. Chevalier wrote:

> There have . . . been strikes on the part of the workmen who wish to share in the profits of speculation and who have demanded higher wages and less work. The demand for higher pay is just since all provisions, all articles of consumption, have risen in price. These coalitions are by no means timid in this country; the English practice of haranguing in public and getting up processions prevails here and the working class feels its strength, is conscious of its power, and knows how to make use of it. The different trades have held meetings in Philadelphia, New York, and other places, discussed their affairs publicly, and set forth their demands. The women have had their meeting as well as the men. That of the seamstresses of Philadelphia attracted notice; Mathew Carey, known as a political writer, presided, assisted by two clergymen.[12]

---

[11] Quoted from Chevalier's *Society, Manners, and Politics in the United States,* excerpts of which appear in *Ideology and Power in the Age of Jackson,* Documents in American Civilization series, Edwin C. Rozwenc, editor (Garden City, N.Y.: Doubleday Anchor, 1964). This statement appears on p. 25.

[12] *Ibid.,* p. 29.

Chevalier goes on to describe the disruptive and violent character of the strikes and disputes and, finally, how the employers increasingly resorted to mechanization to minimize both their dependence on workers and the cost of the conflicts.

Chevalier also perceived, outside the South, at least two classes: "the middle class and the democracy." The middle class, in his view, consisted of manufacturers, merchants, lawyers, and physicians; the democracy included farmers, mechanics, artisans, and workers in general. And between the two classes, conflict in various forms was evident. Thus Chevalier not only recognized the rather conspicuous social stratification prevailing at the time, he grasped as well its longer range social and historical significance. In contrast to Tocqueville's "classless" or one-class society, moving inexorably toward ever greater equality, Chevalier viewed Jacksonian America as the stratified society it was in fact, a society, moreover, whose democratic institutions the newly emerging industrial serfdom would soon put to a severe test. Chevalier's observations, as we shall see, more than Tocqueville's, are borne out both by other contemporary observers and documents and by subsequent historical research.

INDUSTRY AND CLASS CONFLICT

A genuine trade union movement came into being in the United States during the mid-1830's, and expanded rapidly not only in the East but in such western cities as Pittsburgh, Cincinnati, and Louisville. Primarily concerned with raising wages and improving working conditions, many local organizations formed in 1834 a national association called the National Trades' Union. Delegates to the first general convention, representing some 26,000 members in the eastern cities of the United States, formulated a number of working-class resolutions.[13]

Now it is true that this took place a few years after Tocqueville's visit to the United States. During his visit, however, and coinciding with Jackson's election to the Presidency, workingmen's unions, associations, and even political parties appeared in the large eastern cities of Philadelphia, New York, and Boston. Tocqueville makes no mention of these beginnings, which by 1834 had developed into a national working-class

---

[13] See the *Resolutions on the Social, Civil, and Intellectual Condition of the Laboring Classes,* in *The Man* (New York), August 30, 1834, vol. II, p. 357. Or see the excerpts in Rozwenc, pp. 123–127.

association designed to defend and further distinctively working-class interests.[14] The *Resolutions* protested the education of

> the wealthy few at the expense of the industrious many, fostering, by means of Colleges, Universities, Military or Naval Academies, etc., a professional Monopoly of Knowledge, thereby drawing a line of demarcation between the producers of all the wealth, and the other portions of society which subsist upon the fruits of the Working Man's industry.

Thus they were demanding a system of equal and universal education and protesting the very thing Tocqueville deemed impossible under American democracy — aristocratic or elite educational institutions.

The delegates also protested the inequitable distribution of public land that, they argued, belonged to the whole people. They condemned the *sale* of public lands as effectively precluding the workers from land ownership and enabling the wealthy to accumulate and amass wealth in land. They especially protested employing child labor and condemned "the deplorable condition of the male and female children employed in the cotton and woolen manufactories in the country, and the many privations they are subjected to, arising from the early age they are put to work in factories and the enormous length of time allotted for a day's labor." The *Resolutions* not only recommended that the various unions of the country should protest these conditions before their respective state legislatures, but also suggested "that lawful security should be exacted from the proprietors of manufactories, for the education of every child employed by them therein."

Apparently, employers, already at this early date, had perceived the unions as a serious enough threat to their interests to gain the passage of special antiunion legislation. Certain laws of the time treated the organization of trade unions among mechanics as illegal combinations. The *Resolutions* challenged the constitutionality of these laws and demanded their repeal. Finally, the delegates called upon all their fellow workers to strive for legislation that would further their best interests and to inform themselves of their "equal rights and [to] labor to promote the good of the whole community, rather than to confer privileges on a favored few."

In general, workers were in great competition for jobs, particularly the immigrants and Negroes. "During the thirties," writes Harvey Wish, "Irish belligerency blew up into a murderous civil war among canal construction gangs, which brought local militia and even inspired the first

---

14 See Rozwenc's introduction to the *Resolutions,* pp. 122–123.

use of federal troops — Jackson's — in any labor dispute." [15] The frequently jobless Irish and, later, Germans lived in poverty and slums in Boston and New York.

If all this found not the faintest echo in Tocqueville's work, neither did the tendency that some contemporaries, for example, William Leggett of the *New York Evening Post*, recognized as leading to fundamental inequalities. Leggett argued that the acts of special incorporation conduced to a privileged order for it concentrated "all wealth and power in the hands of the few. . . ." [16] To counteract this tendency, Leggett called for something resembling a cooperative movement, a general law of association that would enable the humblest of citizens to

> associate together, and wield, through the agency of skillful and intelligent directors, chosen by themselves, a vast aggregate capital, composed of little separate sums which they could afford to invest in such an enterprise, in competition with the capitals of the purse-proud men who now almost monopolize certain branches of business. [17]

All this is related, of course, to the main omission from Tocqueville's work, an omission that must be regarded as a major flaw. For he missed altogether what Chevalier and others at least glimpsed: the beginnings of urbanization and industrialization, processes so fundamental after all that, in a few decades, they would so transform American society that little or nothing remained of Tocqueville's America.

Even during Tocqueville's visit these fundamental social processes were evident to some observers. George Tucker, for instance, an outstanding American demographer, historian, and economist of the time, noted that industrial occupations and large cities (over 10,000) were expanding at a faster rate than the general population. "It . . . appears," he concluded from his data, "that the increase of those towns [with populations exceeding 10,000] has been nearly the same, from 1830 to 1840, as from 1820 to 1830; and that, in both decennial periods, it exceeds that of the whole population, nearly as 50 to 32. . . ." [18]

Equally important, Tucker found ". . . that the proportion of labour employed in agriculture and commerce had diminished; while that employed in manufactures had, in twenty years [1820–1840] increased

---

[15] Harvey Wish, *Society and Thought in Early America* (New York: David McKay, 1950), p. 317.

[16] See the excerpts in Rozwenc, *op. cit.*, p. 222.

[17] *Ibid.*, p. 225.

[18] *Ibid.*, p. 6, from George Tucker, *Progress of the United States in Population and Wealth in Fifty Years as Exhibited by the Decennial Census from 1790 to 1840* (New York, 1855), abridged.

from 13.7 percent to 17.1 percent of the whole. The positive increase in that time was from 349,506 persons employed in 1820, to 791,749 employed in 1840." [19]

While Tocqueville, mainly as a result of his a priori, developmentally static model of American social structure, underscored the agrarian, commercial character of American society in general and of New England in particular, Tucker's statistics showed that the increase of the manufacturing population was greatest in New England, where it had "enlarged from 21 percent, in 1820, to 30.2 percent in 1840; in which time the same class of population had nearly trebled in Massachusetts, and more than trebled in Rhode Island. In the Southwestern states, alone, the proportion of the agricultural class had increased; in all the others it had diminished." [20]

Manufacturing was growing rapidly and was second only to agriculture, with commerce trailing far behind. According to Tucker's data 1 out of $4\frac{1}{2}$ persons was employed in agriculture while 1 out of $21\frac{1}{2}$, and 1 out of 145 was employed in manufacturing and commerce, respectively. Tocqueville systematically obscured these facts from his own view and that of his readers, an inevitable consequence of both his a priori conception of American society and his predominantly social psychological mode of analysis, which virtually left out economic and other structural conditions and trends. His favoring of social psychological typology and portraiture over structural analysis is evident throughout, but particularly in the striking imprecision and ambiguity of his key concepts and terms, which is true not only of his relatively abstract concepts such as "liberty," and "democracy," but also of his use of "industrial," which often refers to commercial and even agricultural occupations, just as by "worker" he may have meant either an industrial or agricultural worker, or even a small farmer who worked part time for another, bigger farmer.[21]

To summarize, it is relatively clear that in his *Democracy* Tocqueville wrote more as a philosopher of history and less as a methodologically rigorous and empirical historian or social scientist. He conceived a great central historical law and proceeded largely to deduce from that law everything that appeared logically to follow.

The progress of history brought with it an inexorable levelling

[19] *Ibid.*, pp. 7–8.

[20] *Ibid.*, p. 8.

[21] See *Democracy in America,* vol. II (New York: Knopf, 1948), especially pp. 187–192.

tendency, which was necessary, inevitable, providential. The irresistible march of equality meant that all forms of privilege, classes, and social stratification were disappearing and being abolished. To demonstrate this was the purpose of his ideal-type dichotomy, *aristocracy-democracy*. The master trend of history was from one to the other and the United States was, if not actually there, well on the way.

For many reasons probably associated with his aristocratic background, he consistently emphasized the superiority of moral forces, which were both more effective and desirable than economic and technical-industrial forces in shaping and changing a social order. Hence, one encounters throughout his work a predominantly social-psychological conception of society and an overwhelming emphasis on religion, personal morality and law in social change, and good government.[22] His conception also caused him, as we have seen, to overlook the significance of industrial growth and urbanization; for although he traveled in every major American city and himself witnessed some of the early industrial wonders, he never appreciated how industry would "transform his chosen civilization almost overnight." [23] In general, his neglect of material economic developments in favor of moral forces caused him to miss the strategic importance of economic changes in altering political, moral, and intellectual conditions.

And although Tocqueville made much of the possibility of a tyranny by the majority, he never seriously anticipated a tyranny by a minority, which too was related to his ideological outlook and to his neglect of economic conditions; because of this neglect he underestimated the growth and concentration of economic power, the emergence in the near future of financial, industrial, and political elites with immense power over great masses of people. As G. W. Pierson wrote: "With his [Tocqueville's] fears of the mob, and his concern for the atom individual, he did not allow enough for the ingenuity of the designing few, the potential indifference of the many." [24]

TOCQUEVILLE'S MODEL AND RECENT HISTORIOGRAPHY

Recent historical research has, if anything, undermined further the validity of Tocqueville's model and analysis. His conception of an already equalitarian America growing ever more equalitarian was wrong on both

---

[22] George Wilson Pierson, *Tocqueville and Beaumont in America* (New York: Oxford, 1938), p. 762.

[23] *Ibid.*, p. 763.

[24] *Ibid.*, p. 767.

counts. He not only greatly exaggerated the equalitarian character of the Jacksonian era; he failed to see that the main structural trend was away from equality.

Thoroughly wedded to his abstract universal historical law, he saw in America what he wished to see and either ignored or treated as exceptional all phenomena not in accord with his master concept. Thus Tocqueville deceived himself. But he was further deceived by the structure of American society because it appeared and in fact was different in many important respects from the *traditional* stratification system of European society. The differences therefore blinded him to the similarities between America and Europe and to the distinctive strata and classes of American society.

For Tocqueville, America was not only equalitarian; it was essentially agrarian (and only secondarily commercial), and he saw no reason why it should not remain so. No wonder, then, that the great urban and industrial expansion, and the class system peculiar to it, went unnoticed. However, with the great growth of cities, speculative capital, and industry, many settlers traversed the mountains to seek their fortunes in towns as well as in land. The so-called frontier included Cincinnati, Lexington, Pittsburgh, St. Louis, and Louisville. And in all cities one could discern rich and poor, clearly separated residentially and in quality of housing. In the western cities, the well-to-do bought up the choice areas leaving the less desirable ones to the less well-off; in eastern cities, the rich built homes of fine stone and brick and increasingly used white marble "for doorsteps, window sills, lintels, and entire first stories." [25] They decorated their homes with pure silver ornaments and costly imports from Europe.

The conditions, on the other hand, in which working people lived were quite different. In Philadelphia, for example, Matthew Carey, the famous philanthropist, described them as crowded together, fifty-five families in a tenement, without even "a privy for their own use." Edward Pessen cites a more recent study describing the houses of working-class families as "strung along, side to side as boxcars . . . obscured from the street view. . . ." Typically, families lived in a single room "huddled to the rear . . . victims of a parsimonious building policy which meant crowding, noise, inadequate sanitation, lack of facilities for rubbish removal." [26] The Schuylkill, with its fresh water European travelers so

---

[25] Edward Pessen, *Jacksonian America: Society, Personality, and Politics* (Homewood, Ill: Dorsey, 1969), p. 47. I rely heavily in the present discussion on Pessen's work, particularly Chapter 3, pp. 39–58.

[26] *Ibid.*, p. 47.

admired, "went into the homes of the wealthy," Pessen writes, "but not to the working-classes. According to the labor press, the major cities of the nation abounded with dismal alleys, 'the abodes of the miserable objects of grinding poverty.'" And although it may have been perfectly true, as many distinguished foreign visitors besides Tocqueville noted, that one saw few beggars in the street, one could find many "in less public places." Andrews Bell had observed "scores of destitute homeless wretches lying on bulks or under the sheds about the markets of New York and Philadelphia." [27] More generally, Pessen observes that:

> Statistical studies confirmed the rising rates of pauperism and of those too poor to pay a minimal tax. Nor does the evidence indicate that membership in these forlorn groups was swelled by the dramatic failure of eminent men. Rather some poor men became poorer. Imprisonment for debt was also on the rise, in some cities evidently accounting for the majority of men in jail. This abuse was shortly to be outlawed, in large part because its negative effects were felt by businessmen as well as the poor. In the Jacksonian era, however, its main victims were men who owed $20 or less.

Although abject poverty was not characteristic of Americans who were not wealthy, it was not a negligible phenomenon. In 1834, in Boston, more than 5,000 persons received aid annually, according to a labor newspaper edited by the respected George Henry Evans. And Pessen cites Edward Abdy's observation that pauperism was not only increasing in the nation's major cities, but that "there . . . was little reason to hope it . . . could be checked by the judicious application of charity." [28]

Most urban Americans were neither paupers nor debtors, but artisans, mechanics, small businessmen, and not particularly well-to-do professionals. Yet, urban workers lived and worked under extremely trying conditions, bearing no resemblance to the prosperity Tocqueville saw elsewhere. Artisans, whose working day was rarely shorter than that of the farmers, were subject to frequent unemployment and "when they did work, . . . were paid in a paper currency that invariably was not worth its face value. . . ." Pessen continues:

> Quite apart from the depression years labor fared poorly during the Jacksonian era. Most modern studies indicate that real wages stood still during an otherwise exuberant economic surge in the 1830's, at best approximating what they had been at the turn of the century.[29]

---

[27] Cited in *ibid.*, p. 48.
[28] Cited in *ibid.*
[29] *Ibid.*, p. 49.

But if these were the conditions of urban America, perhaps a basic equality was more characteristic of the countryside? Some two-thirds of the American population was engaged in agriculture during the Jacksonian era, and although the available data are not as reliable as one would prefer, they leave no doubt that there were both rich farmers and poor farmers. Farmhands and laborers earned even less than urban workers, and impressionistic evidence indicates that even the independent farmers of moderate success could hardly be described as prosperous. Pessen writes:

> Thomas Coffin's family in New Hampshire worked hard, lived frugally and had little leisure. Ridding the farm of vermin constituted an amusement or form of recreation for the young. A large farm that was regarded as "fairly well improved," located on one of the "better developed farm communities," in Iredell County, North Carolina, characteristically eked out a living, its "produce yielding only a small return for the work involved, while prices of necessities bought were high." Living conditions were indeed discouraging to men who found that their incomes from sales frequently only balanced their purchases. American farmers in the antebellum period were also convinced that their status was low. The "agrarian myth" that romanticized rural life was either unknown to most farmers or disbelieved by them.[30]

It was not, moreover, only "radical" labor leaders who pointed to the real inequalities prevailing in American social life at the time. Conservative Americans did the same, some in personal conversations with Tocqueville who nonetheless remained unshaken in his a priori convictions.

John Quincy Adams told Tocqueville that although citizens in the North had "great equality before the law . . . it simply does not affect our ways of life. There are upper classes and working classes." [31] Peter Duponceau agreed that extreme inequalities, created by money, existed in American society, as did Thomas Hamilton and Chevalier. Hamilton saw rather clearly that the absence of a privileged aristocratic class on the European model did not mean that the United States was a land of equality. And as we have seen, Chevalier suggested that inequalities in wealth were increasing and that this tendency was associated with the emerging urban-industrial society.

Even if one were to take Tocqueville's meaning to be that in America

---

30 *Ibid.*, p. 49.

31 Alexis de Tocqueville, *Journey to America* (New Haven: Yale University Press, 1960), p. 61.

it was not so much equality as equality of opportunity that prevailed, which certainly was not his meaning, this, too, is not borne out by the evidence. When he advanced his thesis on social mobility and wrote: "In America most of the rich men were formerly poor," he was probably further from the truth than J. S. Buckingham, who observed that "the greater number of America's social elite . . . inherit land, or houses, or stock, from their parents." [32] Whether it was Wayne County, Michigan, or Boston, Massachusetts, the rich were the sons of the rich or otherwise privileged.

Generally great differences in styles of life prevailed and social distance separated strata and classes: the old rich shunned the new while both shunned all those below. "Large merchants scorned small, while in a number of cities merchants of any sort would receive neither mechanics nor their children." [33] Even in the newer cities of the West merchants constituted a "distinctively wealthy and socially prominent group." They had their own clubs, segregated themselves residentially and in other ways from others, imitated the older upper classes, lived frequently in "villas," and in general indulged themselves in a most conspicuous display of their wealth. This was also true of the "frontier towns," where, as Richard Wade has shown, "local boosters talked a great deal about egalitarianism in the West, but urban practice belied the theory." [34]

In the East, in Boston for instance, invidious distinctions reached the point where "Women of Society . . . curtsied according to their wealth and circumstances. Not only was seating in theatres arranged according to class, applause was given by class." And although Pessen regards as extreme the view that America was ruled by a small upper class, he notes that the evidence suggests "that wealthy men commanded an inordinate political influence over American society." [35] Historical research in the past twenty years indicates that unusually wealthy men controlled the political parties. The men who supported Jackson, too, were uncommonly wealthy, while Jackson himself, despite his rhetoric about the common man, "filled the Cabinet and high civil service posts with men who possessed unusual wealth and social eminence." [36]

In short, the tendency prevailing in America at the time was quite opposite to that which Tocqueville posited from his abstract thesis. For as

---

[32] Quoted by Pessen, *op. cit.*, p. 52.

[33] *Ibid.*, p. 53.

[34] *Ibid.*

[35] *Ibid.*, p. 55.

[36] *Ibid.*, p. 56.

Pessen has summarized the results of most recent research, the "Jacksonian era witnessed no breakdown of a class society in America. If anything, class lines hardened, distinctions widened, tensions increased." [37] Tocqueville had effectively deluded himself in this crucial respect, never recognizing in America the class society that it was.

[37] *Ibid.*, p. 57. For additional sources on Jacksonian America and the modern Jacksonian controversey, see Pessen's Bibliographical Essay, pp. 352–394. In addition, other relevant sources are:

Nelson Manfred Blake, *A History of American Life and Thought* (New York: McGraw-Hill, 1963).

Carl Bode, ed., *American Life in the 1840's* (Garden City, N.Y.: Doubleday Anchor, 1967).

David Brion Davis, ed., *Ante-Bellum Reform* (New York: Harper and Row, 1967).

Aileen S. Kraditor, *Means and Ends in American Abolitionism* (New York: Pantheon, 1967).

J. R. Pole, ed., *The Advance of Democracy* (New York: Harper and Row, 1967).

George E. Probst, ed., *The Happy Republic* (New York: Harper Torchbooks, 1962).

Harvey Wish, *Society and Thought in Early America* (New York: David McKay, 1962).

II. Tocqueville in England

Introduction

WHEN TOCQUEVILLE VISITED ENGLAND for the first time (1833), his view of that society was highly colored by his *idée mère*. The world democratic revolution, he believed, soon would manifest itself in that country as earlier it had in America and France. His orientation continued to be rural, and he concerned himself mainly with class relations in the countryside and with the "land question." The patterns he had observed in America and France appeared to suggest that some form of agrarian revolution was unavoidable in England.

While still in the United States Tocqueville had learned from John Livingston about the rich landed proprietors of pre-revolutionary America who had lived like English gentry. When, following the revolution, primogeniture was abolished, that class disappeared, which was an important democratic consequence of the revolution. Similarly, issues of land and agrarian class relations in France had culminated in the great revolution. The abolition of the landed aristocracy in both societies diminished the number of great landowners, facilitated the division of land into small holdings, and hence led to the creation of a large class of middle-sized and small landed proprietors. For Tocqueville, as for Jefferson, this class was to be the firm social basis of a liberal-democratic society and polity. Nothing, Tocqueville believed, was more essential to democracy than a large class of small but independent farmers.[1]

---

[1] Cf. Seymour Drescher, *Tocqueville and England* (Cambridge, Mass.: Harvard University Press, 1964), p. 40. This is probably the best study of Tocqueville's view of England and of the impact of English thought and experience on his intellectual development.

The fact, then, that land concentration was so great in England could only mean that an agrarian revolution was imminent. Only after Tocqueville discovered that the great concentration of landed property in England was accepted without either resentment or outrage by all classes of English society, including the poor, did he begin somewhat to revise his opinions. This revision, to be taken up later, he made mainly during his second visit to England (1835). Let us first see how Tocqueville perceived the English aristocracy and the conditions in the countryside and then assess the validity of his observations in light of the present state of our historical knowledge.

4. The English Aristocracy

THE ARISTOCRACY OF ENGLAND was an old and established class and remained so even after opening its ranks to commoners — who thus became aristocrats — and after beginning to share power with the middle classes. In obvious contrast, in France the retention of aristocratic privilege had led to hardening class lines, to great aristocratic arrogance, and, hence, to great hostility toward the nobility by the middle and lower classes. In spite or, more correctly, because of its rigidity and arrogance, the French nobility long before the revolution had become comparatively weak; having alienated itself from the classes below, it was also unable to prevent the extreme centralization of power.

The English aristocracy, on the other hand, had successfully curbed and checked the power of the monarchy. This, after all, was one of the main sources of English liberty, which originated with the aristocracy and afterward was modified and adapted to their needs by the middle classes and their political representatives.

The really important feature of the English aristocracy, however, was not merely the openness of its ranks but the vagueness of its boundaries. One knew where it began, Tocqueville often noted, but not where it ended. Aristocratic qualities and privileges, which in so many other countries were regarded as odious, were not so regarded in England. It was not true, as often had been alleged, that the poor could attain aristocratic station. But rich commoners could realistically aspire to rank, because it was a conspicuous fact that members of this class were actually joining the aristocracy. Thus Tocqueville already now points to a condition that he was to emphasize more than twenty years later in his analysis of class relations under the old regime: it was not their privileges per se that had rendered the French nobility so hateful and detestable, but rather that the bourgeois newcomers could not become really noble. For when the bourgeois bought aristocratic titles, a great barrier still remained between them and the old aristocrats.

The English aristocracy was not based on birth alone, which would have made it an exclusive and closed caste like its French counterpart, but on money. Title and money mixed easily in this society and this development strengthened the aristocracy as compared with the power of both the monarchy and the people. Amalgamation with the upper middle class imparted a unique power and viability to the English aristocracy.

However, even this unique aristocracy, Tocqueville believed at this stage of his thinking, could not be considered invulnerable. After all, one's respect for that class and especially one's hopes for joining it, varied with one's own class position: it made a big difference whether one was a big banker, financier, or owner of a very large landed estate on the one hand, or a small merchant or worker on the other. Clearly, the former felt closer and gave more support to the aristocracy than the latter. One could then after all see a line separating the aristocracy from the middle classes and the people. That line, Tocqueville believed, had revolutionary implications.

The strata having no hope, or almost none, of entering the aristocracy had become more numerous than ever before; Tocqueville imagined that they saw their potential revolutionary power quite clearly. Furthermore, even among those who had a better chance of joining the aristocratic ranks, a large group believed they could arrive faster by another route. In Tocqueville's words: *"L'esprit démocratique, qu'en Europe on pourrait appeler l'esprit français, a fait des progrès effrayants parmi elles."* [1]

Nevertheless, Tocqueville felt that the English aristocracy, supported by the upper strata of the financial and commercial classes, would continue to be in a good position from which to fight for the maintenance of its supremacy—if it could ensure material prosperity to the lower classes. "In order that a man of the people should find himself satisfied in a sphere from which it is almost impossible to leave, it is necessary that he be well off" (30). Tocqueville is concerned with what he regards

---

[1] Alexis de Tocqueville, *Oeuvres Complètes,* Edition définitive publiée sous la direction de J. P. Mayer, tome V, 2, *Voyages en Angleterre, Irlande, Suisse et Algérie* (Paris: Gallimard, 1958), p. 30. Hereafter citations to this work will be indicated simply by the page number in parentheses immediately following the quoted passage. Translations are mine.

as the irresistible revolution of the lower classes, particularly in the countryside. So he adds that the preceding observation is especially true in times "such as ours," of intellectual agitation and moral unrest.

A Frenchman visiting England for the first time, Tocqueville observed, is struck by the ease of the way of life and cannot imagine why the English people should grumble and complain. Here Tocqueville observes that culturally defined needs may come to be regarded as no less vitally important and necessary than natural needs. Relative deprivation may lead to real and profound misery — so that men kill themselves because of evils that to their neighbors appear imaginary. For the English people, lacking what others may regard as luxury is as painful as the lack of clothing and bread to the Russian. As we shall later see, Tocqueville may have erred in viewing the deprivation of the English poor as merely relative.

On balance, Tocqueville felt that the aristocracy could successfully maintain its hegemony by forming a compact body with those strata that had some hope of joining the aristocracy and participating in its privileges. This association might prevent a revolution in England because nothing is harder for the lower orders than to make a revolution by themselves. But they were not entirely alone. One could see evidence of the democratic sentiment among increasing numbers from the upper classes who preferred an apparently shorter route to power and privilege — aligning themselves with the people. One finds, as a result, many men on the people's side whom one would have expected on the other.

Thus, if the aristocracy of the "first order" alienates that of the second, it strengthens thereby the forces of revolution. In a crisis, in which the whole class should be threatened, the "second order" might again make common cause with the first. But then it may be too late for "the revolution will be too far advanced to stop it" (31). If Tocqueville at first believed, influenced by his master idea, that the country was on the brink of a great and violent revolution, his reflections on the relationships among the classes eventually forced him to change his opinion somewhat. He explains this change in the final impressions of his first visit.

If one means by revolution a fundamental change in the legal, political, and social structures of a society and replacing old principles with new, then assuredly England is in a state of revolution. A fundamental element of the English social structure, the aristocratic principle, each day loses some of its force, while the democratic principle increasingly asserts itself and, in all likelihood, will eventually take its place. But if one means by revolution a sudden and violent change, then, "England seems to me not ripe for such an event" (36), Tocqueville concluded from his comparative analysis of English and French institutions.

A peculiarly English condition essential for understanding English society was the *embourgeoisement* of the English nobility. In England an illustrious name was a great advantage and a source of pride to those who bore it. Yet it was not primarily birth but wealth on which the aristocracy was based. For this reason one saw clearly where the aristocracy began but not where it ended. Tocqueville elaborates upon this observation with an example he uses repeatedly. The difference between the respective social structures of France and England could be characterized by examining one word of their respective languages. Gentleman and *gentilhomme* evidently have the same origin; but gentleman is applied in England to every man of high status, whatever may have been the station of his birth, but in France *gentilhomme* is never applied to anyone of non-noble birth. The meanings of the two words of apparently common origin have become as different as the respective societies in which they are used. So different have the meanings become in fact that one cannot translate them simply from one language to another without adding a sociological comment. This seemed to suggest to Tocqueville that:

> The English aristocracy could . . . never engender the violent hatred that in France animated the middle classes and the people against the nobility, an exclusive caste that monopolized all privileges and wounded all sensibilities and at the same time never allowed anyone even to hope that he could enter its ranks (37).

The English aristocracy was a much more open, accessible, and mixed category than its counterpart on the Continent. Those therefore who wished to attack it would have great trouble defining its boundaries. Yet, even this aristocracy, based on wealth in general and not on land alone, was, Tocqueville thought, each day losing its power. How could the universal democratic revolution not convulse this society too? He compared democracy to a sea that rises and retreats only to return again and again with ever greater force, each time gaining new ground. However matters appeared, the future of all European society was democratic; and England, where the "people" were more and more demanding a voice in government, was no exception. Revolutionary passions and ideas might remain dormant for some time to come if the state were prosperous. But without prosperity, Tocqueville felt that the gradual ascendancy of the democratic principle was irresistible. Each day it attacked some new privilege of the aristocracy; it waged a slow war against particulars but the war would surely end in the total destruction of the aristocratic class as a whole.

For Tocqueville, it was the French nobility's closed-caste character and exclusive privileges that had rendered it so hateful to all other classes of French society. Yet, in crisis, those same characteristics led the nobility to defend itself by uniting as one man, "all its members having a certain and definite interest in the protection of the whole" (38). In England, in contrast, the outer limits of the aristocracy were so vague as to be unknown and it was therefore far from constituting a compact body. More, many of its members were sympathetic in some degree with democratic ideas or saw their interests served by the extension of popular powers. On many issues it already appeared as if the House of Peers was on one side and the rest of the aristocrats, together with the people, on the other. The people's camp attacked in unity while the other offered "a divided and often feeble resistance." "The English aristocracy," Tocqueville continues, "will therefore fall less rudely and more slowly than the French, but I think it will fall as inevitably as the latter" (38). One can expect not a rapid and violent change, but a fundamental change nevertheless.

In France the people had been kept for centuries outside the political process and hence ignorant of all that related to the government of a society. Yet, what they had not learned in centuries, they learned rather quickly once the crisis came. Is there reason to believe that what happened in France will soon repeat itself in England? No! argues Tocqueville. In England not only have various liberties prevailed for some time, notably freedom of the press, but the people have long been exposed to democratic and revolutionary ideas. If these ideas have not yet seized the minds of the masses, one can rest confident that they will require some time to do so.

Although Tocqueville did not deny the possibility of a sudden and total subversion, he perceived few grounds for assuming that England would follow France. He was somewhat aware of how much his key idea may have influenced his perception. "It is easy," he wrote, "to notice in England an alarming symptom . . ." (39). What he called the spirit of innovation appeared to be widely diffused among all the classes, which seemed to indicate "the enfeeblement of the aristocratic principle." The self-satisfaction for which the English people formerly had been famous was no longer evident. Now one could discern a spirit of discontent and an excess of contrariness. Tocqueville perceived a critical, "negative," revolutionary disposition, which he very much feared and disliked. This critical spirit always pointed to the evil about it and dreamt of destroying the bad rather than preserving the good. Yet, dangerous though the situation was, this spirit attacked details not, as in France, the foundation of the existing order.

The attack upon the English aristocracy was only indirect; and public opinion was still far from assailing this class and its institutions at the roots — still far from questioning the utility of the aristocracy in general. The majority in fact appeared to be decidedly in favor of maintaining aristocratic principles. Though aristocratic power appeared to have been shaken somewhat, it continued to rest on a firm basis and remained great. Opening its ranks to the very rich ostensibly contributed to the preservation of the aristocracy, which, with other causes, accounted for the wide diffusion of aristocratic ideology throughout English society, particularly among the middle classes. Tocqueville was "singularly struck" by the degree to which the aristocratic principles had penetrated the manners, morals, and customs of the nonaristocratic classes.

Tocqueville felt he had detected among the "people" what he called "an indefinite sentiment of malaise." But what seemed most characteristic of their discontent was that it was not general but specific; that is, they tended to complain of this or that lord or of particular policies but never questioned the very existence of the aristocratic class, as had been the case in France. Nor did one discern in England the violent hatred and envy that in France was still so characteristic of the lower classes toward all above them. Not that such sentiments did not exist at all in English society, but rather to Tocqueville they appeared weak and undeveloped — and might remain so if the aristocracy could avoid a collision with the people.

In England, Tocqueville observed, the typical middle-class man may hate particular aristocrats but not the aristocracy. Indeed, he thoroughly identifies with that class and apes its ways. He not only distrusts the people profoundly but loves the aristocracy, its social honor, and its accoutrements. "He lives in the hope of achieving all this for himself by means of the democratic veneer with which he has covered himself and, while waiting, he gives a livery to his sole domestic whom he calls a footman, and speaks of his relation with the Duke of so and so and of his descent, however remote, from certain noble lords" (40). Aristocratic values and practices were coveted and emulated by the nonaristocratic classes of English society and this was an important basis of its stability.

Unlike his French counterpart, the typical middle-class Englishman preferred the chance to gain for himself some aristocratic luxury and honor, which, rather than the pursuit of equality, is what motivated him. For Tocqueville, evidence of this was not wanting.

Administration, for instance, was in the hands of justices of the peace appointed in each county by the king; all were selected, moreover, from among the landed proprietors. With France and the United States in mind and his belief in the inevitability of democratic revolution, whatever its form, it is no wonder that Tocqueville regarded this arrangement as especially shocking to "democratic sensibilities." What could be more contrary to democratic theory and practice than to have the king select, exclusively from among the gentry, a magistrate and administrator and then turn over to him the direction of local affairs? But middle-class Englishmen, Tocqueville saw with astonishment, were neither shocked nor indignant. Here again complaints brought against the aristocracy were matters of detail and in no sense fundamentally challenged its institutions and privileges. A general feeling that change was necessary seemed nonexistent and the people appeared to resign themselves to a situation in which they were taxed and governed by those whom they had not appointed and who were "not drawn from their ranks" (41).

What appeared, finally, to Tocqueville as the most conclusive evidence that the aristocracy was still quite far from its demise was that, despite the occasional complaints and signs of bitterness against it, the suggestion of destroying that class, even peacefully by changing the inheritance laws, positively frightened every nonaristocratic person who heard it. Preoccupied as he was with the land question and the poor, Tocqueville had suggested changing the law to many of his informants. Everyone who heard the suggestion recoiled. "I have not yet met anyone," wrote Tocqueville, "who was not horrified by this or similar ideas" (41). Public opinion seemed to accept with equanimity the foundation of the aristocracy — the land-inheritance laws. Yet precisely these laws and the concentration of land appeared to Tocqueville as the main source of revolutionary tensions.

THE LAND QUESTION AND THE AGRARIAN POOR
The condition of the poor was for Tocqueville the deepest wound of English society and, hence, its most vulnerable area. The poor were increasing in a "frightening progression." The number of proprietors was diminishing while the number of proletarians was increasing, which

Tocqueville attributed to the land-inheritance laws and to the extreme indivisibility of landed property. In addition, the prevailing tax policy made it extremely difficult for the proprietors to employ the poor. Everything pointed to the indefinite perpetuation and growth of a class of impoverished rural proletarians. And Tocqueville admitted his "extreme surprise" that the possible revolutionary consequences of this fact were little noted. Equally surprising was that agrarian reform, i.e., the division of the land, was a solution that had not captured the public imagination.

The division of land, on the model of France, suggested itself quite naturally to Tocqueville. This had produced in the French countryside a very large, nominally independent *petite bourgeoisie* — a class Tocqueville regarded as indispensable to a democratic society and polity. Parcelling the land, however, had never been either widely or seriously considered by the English, who were rather committed to the principle of large landed estates as the precondition of agricultural efficiency. More, "they seemed still convinced that extreme inequality of fortune is the natural order of things" — an idea that had deep roots among the poor as well as the rich.

Thus with the concentration of land, the great inequalities, and the growing impoverishment of agricultural laborers, England appeared to be in a "critical situation" that from one moment to the next could plunge her into violent revolution — especially if her people were to develop what Tocqueville called the French viewpoint toward their conditions. On the other hand, with the prevailing state of English consciousness, civil war seemed less likely than a relatively peaceful modification of economic and social conditions. Violent revolution was possible but not highly probable. Yet financial crises and increasing poverty, along with agitation for reform, could conceivably bring popular passions to the point of a revolutionary explosion.

In such an eventuality, the greatest danger lay in what Tocqueville perceived as the apparent isolation of the House of Lords — an isolation that rendered them too weak to effectively resist any future movement for change. The only hope for stemming the tide was in bringing them out of their isolation, which probably would not be accomplished until the popular movement had reached such alarming proportions as to push the secondary strata of the aristocracy, and all others having a positive interest in its maintenance, into an alliance with the high nobility. This is no mere dispassionate analysis on Tocqueville's part. One sees clearly where he stood on the issue: "It is to be feared," he wrote, "that the aristocracy will not attempt to oppose by force the irresistible current of new ideas" (43).

During Tocqueville's second visit to England (1835), he modified his views only slightly. The revolution still appeared possible but he saw perhaps more clearly than before the conditions that made it improbable — conditions which he summed up under the heading of the English spirit that contrasted so sharply with the French. The French resented and rejected superiors; they were agitated and restless. To be something they deemed it necessary to destroy that which was above them. The English, in contrast, thought more in terms of rising, attaining a higher level. It seemed as true in 1835 as during his first visit that the rural poor were not developing a French consciousness, without which revolution in the countryside seemed highly unlikely. They demanded no land for themselves. Half the county they lived in could belong to a single proprietor, and yet it would never occur to them that dividing his immense estate, and distributing it among them, could bring to each greater ease and comfort.

Nor did the law of primogeniture generate the discontent one might have expected at the top of the social structure; many remunerative and honorific positions were available to the *branches cadettes* of the aristocratic families. These positions enabled the younger brothers to remain within the ranks of the ruling class and precluded the discontent that might have aligned them with the people. In his conversations with Henry Reeve, Tocqueville learned that the church, the courts, and the army were the three main English institutions whose command posts were manned by the younger sons of the aristocracy. A fourth outlet was the colonial administration and other opportunities in India.

Generally, the very large proprietors appointed the higher functionaries of the established church to highly remunerative positions. The same applied to the courts of law: the wealthy proprietor made a first payment for his son who thereby became a permanent member of the elite. In the army, too, commissions were bought, and the common soldier hardly ever became an officer. Finally, the aristocracy encouraged their sons to seek their fortunes in India where, if one survived the hazards to health — the odds were three to one against it — one was sure to get rich. Reeve agreed with Tocqueville "that the most efficient means of destroying the aristocracy would be to destroy these sources of wealth or to make them accessible to all" (49). Tocqueville therefore concluded that the rear guard of the aristocracy could become the vanguard of the immense, but presently leaderless, army of democracy if, without attacking the large proprietors themselves, one made "life difficult for their sons and brothers" (49).

How do Tocqueville's observations accord with what is now known about the structure and history of English rural society in the 1830's? Remarkably well, one must say, particularly in light of the fact that his stay in England both times was quite brief; and in spite of the fact, one must add, that he relied for his information not on firsthand reports of participant observers but rather on informants far from the scene, usually members of the upper classes who resided in the towns and cities. Apparently Tocqueville interviewed no farmers and never met or spoke with an agricultural laborer.

However, Tocqueville made no mention of the wide and powerful movement of social protest, including riots, arson, and wrecking agricultural machinery (mainly threshing machines) that exploded in the countryside in 1830 and continued sporadically until the middle of 1832 — a movement, moreover, that never assumed the antiaristocratic character he originally would have predicted using his general theory of the democratic revolution.

THE SOCIAL STRUCTURE OF RURAL ENGLAND IN THE 1830'S

Unlike most European countries of the time, England had few peasants — those peasants in the British Isles at the time were to be found mainly in Ireland, Wales, and the Scottish Highlands. In England, however, peasants had become a socially unimportant minority. So although the term "peasantry" was still in use, its meaning was quite different from that on the Continent. In England peasantry referred not to direct family cultivators of their own small plots, but to agricultural wage laborers, who were the typical agriculturalists of rural England and constituted the bottom layer of the social pyramid.[2]

At its apex was the gentry, a very small number of landlords who owned most of the land. However, the members of this class rarely cultivated their own estates directly; nor did they themselves hire rural laborers to do so. Instead, landlords rented their estates to tenant-

---

[2] The present discussion is based on Eric Hobsbawm and George Rudé, *Captain Swing* (New York: Pantheon, 1968). References to this work, the most recent and thorough study of the agricultural uprisings of the 1830's, will hereafter be indicated by *ibid.* and page number only, immediately following the cited passage.

farmers who in turn employed landless, agricultural proletarians to work the land. Moreover, one should not be misled by the term "tenant-farmer" because "what passed for a small farm in England would certainly have counted as a giant farm beside the small holdings of typical peasant economies" (*ibid.*, 24). The rural social structure therefore consisted of three main strata: gentry, farmers, and landless hired laborers, and included, in addition, all the other occupations that

> provided the services necessary to agriculture and village life, not to mention the less numerous professional men who provided those necessary to farmers and gentry; and of course the Church, which went with the Squire. . . . Nor ought we to forget the various rural industries, either domestic and cottage manufactures (such as the straw-plaiting of Bedfordshire) or the small (mainly textile) nuclei . . . fairly widely spread through even the most agricultural counties, with some notable exceptions (*ibid.*, 24).

The division of rural society into three main strata probably prevailed by the middle of the eighteenth century and the transformation of the rural economy from feudalism to capitalism long antedated the industrial revolution. During the revolution, however, very significant changes in rural life took place mainly as a consequence of the famous Enclosure Acts

> which, between 1750 and 1850 turned well over 6 million acres, or something like *one-quarter* of the cultivated acreage from open field, common land, meadow or waste into private fields. . . . Three-quarters of the 4,000 private acts of parliament which thus revolutionised English farming and landscape . . . were concentrated in the 1760's and 1770's, and again during the revolutionary and Napoleonic wars (1793–1815) (*ibid.*, 27).

This together with the fact that the population of England and Wales more than doubled between 1750 and 1840, and that in the 1830's domestic production of grain was nonetheless sufficient for virtually the entire population, was bound to have a profound impact upon rural society.

Industrialization in addition meant, apart from short-term fluctuations, a permanently increasing "demand for food for the growing towns, the rising numbers of non-agricultural workers, and indeed the expanding population in general" (*ibid.*, 27). Nevertheless, the farming communities felt themselves under great pressure that was ultimately expressed in a great uprising of the agricultural laborers.

In the 1830's science and mechanization did not yet account for the immense increase of output in agriculture. Rather it was the large additional areas of land brought under cultivation, the wider use of the best traditional agricultural methods, and, finally, the increasing application of business rationality to farming. Unlike the peasant who typically runs a household and produces for himself and family, the farmer runs a business in which he produces for the market and hopes to profit thereby. In response to the growing market for food, economic rationality and capitalistic agriculture prevailed in the countryside quite some time before Tocqueville first visited England. Both the landlords and the farmers fostered capitalistic agriculture. For the landlord this meant obtaining the maximum rent from the most enterprising farmers, while he himself had little or no direct contact either with farming or with the market.

Farmers were not a homogeneous stratum. There were small and large ones, the latter growing at the expense of the former being the most pronounced tendency. The large tenant farmer, as foreign visitors often noted, did not work and was therefore confused with the landlord. Tocqueville must be included among such visitors for he probably did not recognize, at least not clearly, the big farmers as a distinct non-aristocratic stratum. They constituted a rural middle class despite the superficial aristocratic characteristics they might have assumed; for their interests were distinct from both the gentry and the rural proletarians.

The farmers resented most the twin burdens of tithes and taxes. The tithes made the clergy the most unpopular section of the upper classes and also made it possible, as we shall see, for the farmers to ally themselves at least occasionally with the laborers. The tax, on the other hand, particularly the Poor Rate, divided the farmers and other members of the middle class against themselves, as the Rate fell equally on all "whether they employed labor or not" (*ibid.*, 34). But the Poor Rate also opposed the farmers to the laborers who, since the institution of the Poor Law of 1795, were guaranteed a minimal subsistence. The Poor Rate was especially advantageous to the big farmers who employed many laborers and who could increasingly pay less than a living wage, fully confident that the difference would be made up from the local tax funds.

THE RURAL PROLETARIAN

By the time Tocqueville first visited England, traditional labor relations between servant and master had been largely superseded by rural wage laborers and employers, standing in a strictly market relationship to each other. Landless wage laborers, subject to the vicissitudes of the labor market, were a significant and ever-growing class. The "callous cash nexus," to use Marx's modification of Carlyle's phrase, increasingly dissolved the older "idyllic" relations, while the

> farmhand became essentially a casual laborer, hired and dismissed at will, and lacking even the guarantee, as he set out in a misty dawn, that he would return home that night with any earnings at all. The decline in payments in kind reduced him, except at harvest when every hand was needed, to nothing but a precarious cashwage, which might or might not cover his modest subsistence costs. The many local variations do not disturb this sombre generalization (*ibid.*, 44).

The "relentless proletarianization" of agricultural labor Hobsbawm and Rudé attribute to several causes — economic, social, and institutional. The expansion of agriculture, which was mainly in cereal crops, minimized the need for a year-round work force and maximized the need for seasonal labor. But two other economic factors were even more important: rising farm produce prices and expanding pools of unemployed labor. Under the former condition "it would obviously pay a farmer to sell as much of his produce on the market as he could, paying his labourers cash and letting them buy their own food; or in other words throwing the burden of inflation on them" (*ibid.*, 45). And with an increasing reserve army of unemployed, cheap labor was almost always available and farmers therefore saw no point in paying good wages to assure the availability of a labor supply for the harvest season, a time of peak demand.

Accompanying the economic changes were social ones, mainly a widening social and financial chasm between farmer and laborers so that the farmer was less and less inclined to work beside his hired man or socialize with him. The laborers, on the other hand, encouraged by rapid social change and the high wages of the early war years, also increasingly resisted the "traditional discipline of the domestic servant" and sought their independence. They soon found, however, that their separation from the master left them far from independent, rather defenseless, powerless, and humiliated by the "traditional troubles of the poor" (*ibid.*, 46).

While farmers sought to pay the lowest wages possible, laborers were confronted by unemployment, underemployment, and rising prices for provisions. However, tradition and custom dictated that a laborer's income, though quite modest, should be sufficient for subsistence. The solution imposed during the 1790's, when hardship was especially acute,

Hobsbawm and Rudé call "a disastrous alternative to the simple increase in basic wage-rates." The rulers of the countryside

> following the example of the magistrates of Berkshire in conference at Speenhamland, decided to subsidise low wages out of local rates, in cases where the labourers' family income fell below the subsistence level, either because the price of bread was too high or the number of children too large. The "bread and children" scale, though never law, was almost universally adopted.
>
> For the next forty years the "Speenhamland system" in one form or another, hung like a millstone round the necks of all rural classes in southern England. The "Poor Law" was no longer something to fall back on in times when a man could not earn his living, it became the general framework of the labourer's life. The distinction between worker and pauper vanished (*ibid.,* 47).

The aim of the so-called Speenhamland system was not, of course, primarily humanitarian. It was a "solution" peculiarly suited to the rulers of the countryside who wished to be both capitalists and traditionalists, who wanted a free market of goods and services "but only to the extent that suited nobles, squires and farmers; they advocated an economy which implied mutually antagonistic classes, but did not want it to disrupt a society of ordered ranks" (*ibid.,* 47). Speenhamland was therefore designed to prevent great social unrest "without raising the market rate of wages" (*ibid.,* 50).

Under these circumstances, laborers became demoralized paupers and the distinction between laborer and pauper blurred. They could neither rise above the relief level nor fall below it. Farmers paid as little as they dared, knowing that the parish would provide the supplement. They devoted their most rational calculations to obtaining a "maximum subsidy for their wage-bill from the rest of the ratepayers. Labourers, conversely, were encouraged to do as little as they possibly could, since nothing would get them more than the official minimum of subsistence" (*ibid.,* 51). Demoralization and declining productivity inevitably resulted and the guardians of the "old poor law" responded to the "rising poor rates and falling productivity . . . by giving the vicious spiral another twist. The poor were starved even further. Between 1815–20 and 1830–35 the English poor law expenditure per head of the population diminished by almost a third, and as a percentage of the national income almost by half. What this meant is that the subsistence minimum of the 1790's, itself hardly on the generous side, was progressively whittled away" (*ibid.,* 51). These and other events paved the way to the 1830 uprisings.

The upper classes, however, were probably not aware of the degree to which their policy was creating conditions of rebellion. And the impoverished laborers, for their part, were sure that both justice and authority were on their side and that King and Parliament would soon right what was obviously wrong and unjust. Far, then, from making democratic, equalitarian, or other revolutionary demands, or even couching them in such terms, they remained at all times within the traditional framework. Indeed, the laborers and the other village poor were not, as Tocqueville correctly noted, antiaristocratic; nor were they radically equalitarian. Quite to the contrary, the essence of their demands was a call for restoring the *status quo ante* in which they were subaltern and unequal but in which they nonetheless had certain definite human rights. In these terms Tocqueville also correctly recognized that the rural poor had no "French consciousness," as he called it.

Tocqueville was probably wrong, however, in making light of the poverty and hardships of the English rural poor and in regarding their deprivation as merely relative. Answers to queries circulated by the Poor Law Commission, among them a question on the grievances that led to the 1830 riots, showed again and again that the laborers were suffering from more than merely relative deprivation. The respondents, who were "normally clergymen, overseers of the poor and others not notably identified with the labourers," all confirmed that poverty, degradation, and desperation were almost universal. The respondents consistently emphasized the distress accompanying unemployment, low wages, harsh treatment of laborers, and the like. "Fear of winter," particularly with inadequate subsistence, was still another reason given for the 1830 riots. And after the poor harvests of the immediately preceding years, 1828 and 1829, the latter being "an entirely disastrous year, as bad . . . as 1817," the fear was altogether justifiable. In the words of Hobsbawm and Rudé, "the labourers must have faced the spring of 1830 with the memory of cold, hunger and unemployment, and the reflection that another winter like the last was more than flesh and blood could bear" (*ibid.*, 85).

At the same time this is not to suggest that this very real deprivation was a sufficient cause of the uprising. Nor even that the areas in which poverty and hardship were greatest were necessarily those where the riots broke out first. No doubt the revolutions taking place across the Channel at the time (1830) had some influence upon the rural proletarians, but it was indirect, i.e., mediated by the rural and smalltown middle classes. And if the revolutions in France and Belgium were a minor factor in precipitating the uprising, they left no distinctive marks upon it. For while the revolutions occurred during British elections in which the Left, inspired by events on the Continent, was successfully challenging

Tory rule, the political issues raised were rather remote from the interests of the rural proletarians and their plight and, accordingly, were not reflected in their movement.

The important point for our purposes, therefore, is that when discontent finally erupted in the countryside, the actions and demands of the protesters and rioters bore none of the earmarks of what Tocqueville conceived as the rising tide of democracy. There was little, if anything, about the rebellious activities of these rural proletarians that one could justifiably describe as a manifestation of Tocqueville's universal democratic-equalitarian revolution.

First, who were the main targets and victims of the rash of arson, burning of ricks and barns, and wrecking of threshing machines? Although the farmers frequently entered into collusion with the laborers against both the landlords and the clergy, and attempted, in characteristically middle-class fashion, to turn the laborers' rising to their own account, the laborers, themselves, more often than not, directed their wrath against the farmers, not the gentry. And what did the laborers demand? Employment, higher wages, and the disuse of threshing machines and other agricultural machinery, which, under the circumstances, contributed to their joblessness. They made no demands that challenged aristocratic authority and exhibited no notable antiaristocratic sentiment.

When the laborers turned their attention to the gentry, it was at the suggestion of the farmers, who sought thereby both to deflect the laborers' wrath from themselves (a wrath, incidentally, that never resulted in the death of a single landlord, farmer, or overseer) and to further their own interests. The farmers thus gave assurances that they would be happy to raise wages if only their rents, tithes, and taxes were reduced. For "how else could they afford to raise . . . wages?" (*Ibid.*, 104.) In this way an uneasy and very temporary alliance was formed between farmer and laborer against squire and parson to relieve the farmer of his financial burdens so he would more easily and readily pay higher wages. Repeatedly the farmers promised to raise wages if the laborers would help them secure reduced rents, tithes, and taxes.

The magistrates, on the other hand, most often of aristocratic background, frequently sympathized with the laborers and acknowledged the justice of their cause. They expressed the opinion publicly that the landlords should do their utmost to comply with the demands by discontinuing the use of threshing machines, by raising wages, and by encouraging their tenants, the farmers, to do the same. Even where the parson or landlord became the prime target, the demands were invariably nonrevolutionary. The laborers, far from being radical, revolutionary, or antiaristocratic, were quite apolitical, confining themselves to a few rudimentary economic demands. More, they were fighting for what they no doubt regarded as their traditional and natural rights and were sure that the "King and God himself" were on their side (*ibid.*, 249).

Thus the aims of these rebels and the character of their movement were not at all what Tocqueville would have anticipated in accordance with his theory of the universal democratic revolution. The rebels never questioned the system of land tenure; they were not peasants and hence demanded no land. Instead, their demands were precisely those one would expect from landless proletarians working under conditions of capitalistic agriculture — namely, a living wage and an end to rural unemployment. Even the Enclosures never became an important issue and accounted for only an infinitesimal percentage of the riots.

Thus despite his rather good grasp of several aspects of English rural society, Tocqueville continued, under the influence of his general theory, to mislead himself well into his second visit: some antiaristocratic revolution, however peaceful, was probably unavoidable. And although he did perceive both the great concentration of land and the proletarianization of labor, it is probably equally true that he had no real appreciation either of the complexity of the social structure of the countryside or of the extent to which capitalism already dominated English agriculture. That capitalism had wrought significant changes in English rural life is an insight Tocqueville could have gained only with the greatest difficulty, given his general lack of appreciation of the role of economic conditions in effecting social change.

Similarly, when he eventually gives some attention to England's urban-industrial conditions, he fails to appreciate that he is witnessing the emergence of what was to become a master trend in western society — capitalist industry. His interpretation is the one we have already encountered in *Democracy in America,* in the famous chapter on the manufacturing aristocracy in which he incorporated his observations of the English industrial system in 1835. Industrial serfdom, he believes, is a "monstrous exception" to an otherwise universal law. But before turning to his observations of industrial conditions, one should review some of his other impressions, particularly about the contribution of the aristocracy to the English form of liberty.

IRELAND IN 1835

The English aristocracy in Tocqueville's comparative perspective was essentially good. Its open ranks and willingness to share power indicated, on balance, that it was likely to survive, not perish, at the hands of the lower orders. It was the outstanding concrete case that most closely approximated the perfect ideal type that Tocqueville had in his head. In his dichotomy of good and bad aristocracies, conceived as opposite ends of a continuum, the English case came very close to the former. Ironically, however, this same aristocracy had also established itself not far from home and had produced an odious caricature of itself with almost unimaginably brutalizing consequences for its subjects, the Irish people. Surely, the Irish case belonged somewhere near the other end of the continuum. And, of course, this held a special interest for Tocqueville as it helped him think through the failures of the French nobility of the old régime — a problem that in all probability had already begun to engage his thoughts.

This probability is suggested by the fact that in 1836 he discussed the problem in an article he wrote for the *London and Westminster Review*. This article, written at the request of John Stuart Mill, was titled "Political and Social Conditions of France, First Article," and may be regarded as a dress rehearsal for his mature work, *The Old Regime and the French Revolution,* written some twenty years later. In the original article Tocqueville underscored the alienation of the French aristocracy from all other classes and contrasted it with its English counterpart that so successfully maintained both its rapport with the other classes and its supremacy over them. In this respect the French aristocracy was like the one that ruled Ireland; for it, too, always remained foreign, standing "in the midst of the people as strangers favored by the prince, rather than as leaders and chiefs." [3]

What struck Tocqueville immediately upon his arrival in Dublin were the sharp contrasts between wealth and poverty and degradation. One saw either magnificent palaces or small, miserable huts. In his notes on his visit to the poorhouse and the university in Dublin (probably Trinity College), he records what he regards as the most hideous and disgusting manifestations of poverty. Between 1,800 and 2,000 paupers were received in the poorhouse daily.

A very long room filled with women and children whose infirmities or age prevent them from working. On the floor paupers lying pell-mell like pigs in the mire of their pen. One finds it difficult not to step on one of the half-nude bodies. In the left wing [is] a smaller room, filled with old and infirm men. They sit on wooden benches, all turned in the same direc-

---

[3] Quoted in Seymour Drescher, *Tocqueville and England* (Cambridge, Mass.: Harvard University Press, 1964), pp. 118–119.

tion and huddled together as if in the pit of a theatre. They neither speak, nor move, nor look at anything; nor do they appear to be thinking. They do not expect, fear, or hope for anything from life.[4]

As he left the poorhouse, Tocqueville saw two paupers pushing a small closed wheelbarrow; they were going to the homes of the rich to get their garbage and bring it to the poorhouse to make soup. Then he proceeded to the university with its "immense and magnificent garden maintained like that of a great landed proprietor." Thus the poorhouse and the university, the hut and the palace were altogether representative of the shocking extremes of Irish society.

In Ireland, Tocqueville saw the bitter fruit of conquest — religious and national hatred. This society contained all the abuses of aristocracy with none of its advantages. The differences in political opinion, religion, and nationality and, finally, the extremes in the material conditions of life, made the aristocrats and their subjects strangers and enemies. Here was a land naturally generous, but whose best yield never reached the people. They never tasted their own grand harvests, which were sent instead to England; they raised fine beef but ate only potatoes. This tragic condition of the Irish people could be attributed to the nature of their rulers — which led Tocqueville to reflect on the fundamentally different consequences of two different types of aristocracy, the English and the Irish, or the best and the worst.

The origin of the first was lost in the obscurity of past centuries. Because no great differences existed from the very beginning between the aristocracy and the people, they had good rapport and mixed easily. The bonds were eventually strengthened even more by the interests the aristocracy had in uniting with the people to withstand the central power. In this situation, the greater the well-being and enlightenment of the people, the more assured was the aristocracy of its existence — a respected, not resented, existence. And the more it was respected, the more certain were the people of preserving their possessions and pleasures. Sharing the same language, morals, and religion with the people, the aristocracy could hardly be regarded as a stranger. Given the favorable circumstance that in England the middle classes rose gradually in importance and came by degree to participate in the power and privileges of the ancient aristocracy; that, correspondingly, money replaced birth as a

---

[4] Tocqueville, *Oeuvres Complètes*, p. 97. Further citations to this volume will again be indicated by the page number in parentheses immediately following the quoted and translated passage.

means of sharing the privileges of the few; that this favored the wealth of all as it led to a "universal effort, a contention among all for the acquisition of well-being and wealth"; that, finally, this nation became an immense commercial center providing untold opportunities that led to all the rest — given all this, and one understands why the poor have hope and rest content with their lot. In short, look at England and you will see a society in which

> the higher classes are more splendid, enlightened, and wise; the middle classes wealthier, and the poor better off than elsewhere; the state is as firm in its designs as if it were governed by a single man and as powerful and strong as if it were based on the will of all the citizens; the people submit to the law as if they made it themselves and order reigns as though it were imposed by a despot; it is a society, finally, in which each man, content with his fate, is proud of his country and of himself (132).

Ireland was a point for point contrast. The origin of its aristocracy, now a ruling caste, was known: it established itself by conquest, and at a time when its civilization was relatively advanced while "the vanquished one was still in a state of semi-barbarism." What emerged was a society comprised of two categories of men with a great material and cultural chasm between them; two classes of men, dissimilar and unequal, each with its own religion, language, morals, and customs. Between the classes there was no rapport but rather alienation and mutual enmity. What characterized the ruling caste was not noblesse oblige but naked oppression; and the subjects soon lost all hope, finding themselves content when they had just enough to keep from perishing.

Thus, in England and Ireland one saw perhaps the best and the worst social systems based on the principle of aristocracy. Both, for Tocqueville, were extremes and the principle, therefore, should not have been judged by either.

This study in contrasts did not blind him, however, to those in England itself. There he saw quite clearly not only that wealth in general was the basis of power and privilege but that money in particular had superseded land in this respect. The whole of English society was based on money: one needed to be rich to be a minister because the position obliged him to spend more than he received from the state; one needed money to become a member of Commons because the costs of electioneering were enormous; one needed money to become a justice of the peace, lord-lieutenant, high sheriff, mayor, overseer of the poor — since all these positions were nonremunerative; one needed money to become a lawyer, a judge, or a clergyman, as the education leading to these professions was extremely expensive. Even to be a litigant one needed to be rich; for he who could not pay bail went to prison. Tocqueville wrote: "There is no country in the world where justice, this fundamental need of the people, is more a privilege of the rich" (63).

Money was the key to all the rest. The cult of money had so penetrated the values of the people that they even conceived of a man's worth in these terms: "he is worth five-thousand pounds [*sic*] a year." Money had become everything. But what did this mean for those who did not have it? Tocqueville wrote:

> The English have left the poor only two rights: to be subject to the same legislation as the rich and to become equal to them by acquiring equal wealth. Yet these two rights are more apparent than real since it is the rich who make the law and who create, for their own profit and benefit and for those of their children, the principal means of acquiring wealth (63–64).

CENTRALIZATION

Already during his first visit to England Tocqueville was preoccupied with the negative consequences of the highly centralized bureaucratic administration of his own country, and he was aware that England had so far avoided such a course. English liberty, he felt, was as much a function of its decentralized administration as of its unique aristocracy, although, of course, the two phenomena were intimately related. Sir John Bowring, a philologist and economist influenced by Bentham, had given Tocqueville an idea he later elaborated in *Democracy:* "We have a centralized government," Bowring told him, "but not a centralized administration" (31). Generally, Tocqueville's informants agreed with him that a centralizing tendency, however slight, could be noted in England; but they minimized the danger of this becoming a dominant trend in England. Tocqueville thus developed a more balanced view of the question after his conversations with these informants, notably John Stuart Mill — conversations that revealed differences between the two thinkers.

Mill granted in a conversation with Tocqueville that the current trend seemed to be toward centralization. When asked, however, whether this frightened him, Mill replied that it did not because he was confident that it would not go too far. Mill was confident because centralization had been most foreign to the English spirit — a spirit that had never led to what Mill called general ideas. If the English have devised a system based on the separation of administrative functions, they have done so not by design but because they find it difficult to conceive of general ideas in matters of government as in all others. The English spirit has traditionally encouraged autonomy and freedom of action. The idea of subjecting people to a routine deemed more useful by those in power but not by the people themselves has spread but little in England.

As Mill develops his views, one sees an important difference between his conception and that of Tocqueville. For Tocqueville, decentralization essentially meant provincial and local autonomy. Thus he tended to equate local autonomy in America and England and assigned little or no importance to the fact that one was based on the principle of democracy and the other on the principle of aristocracy. For Mill, on the other hand, the question of power and which class held it was paramount. "We attack the existing communal and provincial institutions," he told Tocqueville, "because they serve as instruments of the aristocracy . . ." (53). And the power taken from the aristocrats was then vested in the central government simply because no other institutions existed in which to vest it. If the local communities and the counties had been organized on democratic principles, they would have been left quite alone. When Tocqueville asked in reply, "What you call the English spirit, is it not the aristocratic spirit?" — Mill acknowledged that it was an important question he had not yet thought about. As the proposition suggested by Tocqueville now stood, however, it required modification: *"Car l'esprit anglais me paraît autre chose encore que l'esprit aristocratique"* (54).

Both men nevertheless influenced each other. Mill eventually became committed to the small social and political unit as a bulwark against tyranny. Tocqueville, on the other hand, came to believe that the evil effects of centralization could be mitigated by several processes similar to those he saw operative in England at the time.[5]

There were then two opposing forces at work, Tocqueville believed. First was the *"centralizing mania"* emanating from the so-called democratic party. In that quarter passions and motives could be discerned not unlike those in France of 1789: a contempt for institutions that had come down from the Middle Ages and a hatred for the aristocrats who had preserved and used these institutions for their own advantage. In a word, the general, democratic, revolutionary tendency was to see only abuses in the prevailing system. But for this tendency to win, it had to overcome another force, at least equally strong — the English spirit of independence.

---

[5] For a fuller discussion of this point see Drescher, *op. cit.*, p. 80.

For Tocqueville, the real test of the goodness of institutions was not whether they guaranteed the individual's security and happiness, but rather whether the institutions provided each individual with the means of assuring these for himself. The first was the French way; the second, the English. Only the second was compatible with political liberty and thus capable of producing good citizens and men. When he visited Birmingham and Manchester and recorded his impressions of the wretched conditions of the industrial workers, he never suspected that a new socio-economic system was emerging that would increasingly separate large masses from the most strategic means of assuring their own security and happiness.

5. Industry and Workers

IN 1835 ENGLAND WAS the most advanced industrial society in the world, and Manchester was the English city in which modern industry assumed its most representative form. Although Tocqueville did eventually visit Manchester, his first contact with English industrial conditions was in Birmingham, a city characterized by economic and industrial diversity — old and new modes of production, existing side by side. Even Birmingham, however, struck him as unique, without analogy in the other provincial cities of England. The capitalistic spirit, a get-rich-quick attitude, was much in evidence as was the English industrial intelligence, *"à la manière des Américains."* To Tocqueville, the city appeared as one immense workshop, forge, and boutique. One saw only busy men, in a great hurry, their faces blackened by smoke; and one heard only industrial noises, the pounding of hammers, the hissing of steam. Everything was dirty and dark, like a mine of the New World from which nevertheless "there issues forth each instant silver and gold" (67).[1]

Tocqueville only observed the industrial workers from afar, spoke personally to none, and relied, as later in Manchester, on middle- and upper-class informants for information about what he called the social, moral, and political condition of the working classes. Tocqueville learned from his conversations that the petitions and other political pressures of both the manufacturers and the workers of Birmingham and Manchester had

---

[1] Alexis de Tocqueville, *Oeuvres Complètes,* Edition définitive publiée sous la direction de J. P. Mayer, tome V, 2, (Paris: Gallimard, 1951–   ), p. 67. Further citations to this volume will be indicated by the page number in parentheses immediately following the quoted and translated passage.

been instrumental in gaining the Reform Bill of 1832. He also learned that although the people of Birmingham presently participated but little in politics, they had become aware of their potential power. A lawyer named Carter conveyed to Tocqueville his uneasiness about the existence in Birmingham of a large working-class population of some 150,000, close to the capital and with immediate access to an immense supply of guns and other military weapons. In fact, during the agitation for the Reform Bill, the people had threatened to march on London if the Bill were not passed, and the arms manufacturers had been prepared to make guns available.

There were signs, then, that the workers were becoming a political force, even if in this particular instance they had threatened to fight for interests not directly their own. (The English workers themselves would have to wait another thirty-five years to gain the vote).

From Birmingham Tocqueville traveled to Manchester where he saw large-scale industry in its most developed form producing textiles, cotton, iron, copper, and steel. With its large port, Manchester was favorably placed to receive raw materials from abroad and to send its products to all points of the globe. Three canals and a railroad made it possible to transport rapidly the city's products to all parts of England; and as the largest coal mines in the country were located nearby, thus providing low-cost power for the machine-run industry, the city was advantageously situated in virtually all respects to meet the requirements of developing industry.

The "head" of this great industrial complex was English capital with its "love of gain," while the "body" Tocqueville described in terms common to both the early conservative and socialist critiques of the emerging industrial system. The polarities of the new system, and the human cost it entailed, did not escape Tocqueville:

> Among the workers, there are men who come from the area of the country where human needs have been reduced almost to those of a savage, and who can work for a very low wage, thus forcing other workmen, who need to compete for work, to do the same. Hence, the *réunion des avantages* of a poor people and a rich one, of an enlightened and an ignorant one, of civilization and barbarism (78).

Tocqueville records his astonishment that this city, already having attained a population of 300,000, continued to grow at a prodigious rate. He does not, however, attach any long-range significance to the fact. He explicitly compares Birmingham and Manchester but gives no indication of awareness that the former represents the past and the latter, the future.

In Birmingham, the working population lived predominantly in single-family houses; in Manchester a large mass of tenants was typically crammed together in the same house, with many occupying the damp, hot, and foul cellars. In Manchester one saw stagnant water, streets poorly paved or unpaved, and in general little space for human well-being — a few large capitalists, thousands of poor workers, and a small middle class. In Birmingham, there were very few large capitalists but many small ones. In Manchester, the workers were assembled by the thousands in single factories, but in Birmingham the workers worked for themselves or in small workshops with their masters. In Manchester, women and children were widely employed in the industry; not so in Birmingham.

Tocqueville also saw the greater "separation" of the classes in Manchester as compared with Birmingham. But he asks "Pourquoi?" He is not sure of the answer. His critical reflections may be read as an indictment of capitalist industry:

> Raise your head and all around you will see the immense palaces of industry. You will hear the noise of furnaces and the hissing of steam. These vast structures prevent either light or air from penetrating the human dwellings they dominate; . . . here the slave, there the master; there the wealth of a few, here the misery and poverty of the greatest number; there the forces of production organized for the profit of a single man, something which society has not yet learned to do for its profit; here the individual, more feeble, debilitated, and destitute than in a wilderness; here the effects, there the causes (81).

Covering the city was a thick black cloud of smoke through which the sun appeared as a disc without rays; and there is no mistaking Tocqueville's indignation when he observes that it is in this "incomplete day that 300,000 human creatures labor ceaselessly" (81). In this and in other passages Tocqueville's critique of industrial society may be seen in its most unambiguous form. Describing Manchester in 1835, he writes:

> It is in this foul drain that the largest stream of human industry originates and flows out to fertilize the whole world. From this filthy sewer, comes gold. It is here that humanity attains its most perfect development and its most brutish; here civilization works its miracles and civilized man is turned almost into a savage (82).

Having been told by a Mr. Connel, one of the largest manufacturers of Manchester, that each of his 1,500 workers worked about sixty-nine hours a week, Tocqueville asks: "What kind of being will a man necessarily become when he does the same thing for twelve hours a day, every day of his life except Sunday?" (82n)

In addition, Tocqueville was aware of some other characteristics of contemporary capitalist industry — the general tendency for wages to fall, for example. More efficient processes of production were rendering human labor less necessary, increasing the competition among workers, and thus depressing the price of labor. Capitalist industry also tended increasingly to employ women and children — in Mr. Connel's factory they were three-quarters of the work force: "a system destructive of education and dangerous for family morality but a necessary consequence of the fact that these manufactures do not require a large deployment of material forces and that the labor of women and children is sufficient, it being less costly than the labor of men" (83).

Yet, despite all he saw, Tocqueville believed that Birmingham, *not* Manchester, would be the rule in the future: open classes, flexible class lines, and diverse modes of production, side by side. This is borne out by the view he expressed in the second volume of his *Democracy* (1840): not a new form of industrial servitude will win the day but a great equality, and even a greater dignity of labor. But there still remained what Drescher so aptly called the "nagging problem" of the poor minority.[2]

Tocqueville remained opposed to legislation granting the poor a right to relief. The old, the sick, the insane, and the orphans were entitled to public charity but the workers and other poor would have to learn to help themselves. The fact is that just as Tocqueville did not see the direction of socio-economic developments, he did not appreciate the scope and depth of working-class unrest and protest in England — or even in France for that matter. It was as late as 1845 that he made his first reference to "vague and mad theories," that is, socialism; and probably he had read the socialists, e.g., Owen, Saint-Simon, Fourier, Louis Blanc, only after 1843.[3]

By 1847 the unstable situation in France was becoming increasingly clear. Now Tocqueville was prepared, although for strictly pragmatic reasons, to suggest reforms in response to working-class agitation. The potential explosiveness of the situation was quite evident but the only hope he held out for preventing the revolution was certain moderate political reforms.

---

[2] See his excellent discussion in *op. cit.*, pp.138–151.

[3] *Ibid.*, p. 141.

With the convulsions of 1848 Tocqueville became more convinced than ever before that previous revolutions were phases in a permanent revolution. He soon realized that weak reforms could not prevent the greatest social upheaval of his time. What made the revolutions of 1848 inevitable, in his view, were the prevalence and rampancy of revolutionary ideas. Socialism, he believed, was the fundamental issue of the February revolution. Even now, however, he wanted to confine it to the political level, and hoped that political participation would satisfy the workers. In these terms he wanted to consolidate and fulfill the promises of 1789, but not go beyond them, because "socialism," he firmly believed, would certainly abolish liberty altogether. "Socialism," not capitalism, was the "new form of servitude" he feared.

So, as will become more evident in the following chapter, Tocqueville was evading the implications for liberty of the actually emerging socioeconomic system. He continued to believe in the 1850's as in the 1830's that "private property and economic independence were a . . . precondition of genuine political activity on the part of the citizen."[4] But this could only mean that the industrial workers were not to be citizens. Drescher is therefore quite correct when he writes that to the very end Tocqueville's "moral vantage point was fundamentally and narrowly that of the proprietary class to which he belonged."[5] Yet, his analysis as such of the revolutionary events of 1848 was remarkably similar to that of Karl Marx. It should therefore be illuminating to compare the respective analyses of these two extraordinary thinkers.

---

[4] *Ibid.*, p. 148.
[5] *Ibid.*, p. 150.

III. *Sociology of Revolution*

6. Tocqueville and the Revolutions of 1848

IN THE NOW FAMOUS OPENING to his *Eighteenth Brumaire*, Karl Marx wrote: "Hegel remarks somewhere that all facts and personages of great importance in world history occur, as it were, twice. He forgot to add: the first time as tragedy, the second as farce." [1] The men of 1848, it was clear to Marx, were largely parodying the men of 1789. Indeed, the tradition of the past weighed heavily upon all the actors in the revolutionary drama and this fact among others was important for understanding the course of the revolution and its ultimate failure.

The imitation of the past did not obscure from Marx, as it had largely from the actors themselves, the original meaning of the events of 1848: the February revolution and even more so the battle of June constituted the first great confrontation between the two main classes of the modern economic system — the bourgeoisie and the proletariat.

Tocqueville also perceived the parody but to him it seemed rather "like a bad tragedy performed by provincial actors." [2] "In this case," he

---

[1] Karl Marx and Frederick Engels, *Selected Works,* vol. I (Moscow: Foreign Languages Publishing House, 1950), p. 225.

[2] *The Recollections of Alexis de Tocqueville,* translated by Alexander Teixeira de Mattos and edited by J. P. Mayer (London: The Harvill Press, 1948), p. 57. References to this work will hereafter be cited by the page number in parentheses immediately following the quoted passage. This translation of Tocqueville's *Souvenirs* deals with the revolutions in France of 1848 and the period just before the coup d'etat of Louis Napoleon. Tocqueville wrote these memoirs during the period beginning in July 1850 and ending in September 1851. This work in particular begs for comparison with Marx's *Class Struggles in France 1848–1850* and his *Eighteenth Brumaire of Louis Bonaparte.* Other studies that have either suggested or made comparisons of Tocqueville and Marx are: H. J. Laski, "Alexis de Tocque-

continues, "the imitation was so evident that the terrible originality of the facts remained concealed beneath it" (56). "The men of the first revolution were living in every mind, their deeds and words present to every memory . . . ; it seemed to me throughout as though they were engaged in acting the French Revolution, rather than continuing it" (57).

With the revolutions of 1848, Tocqueville increasingly relied on the concept of class in analyzing *contemporary* French society. Classes, their interests, and their relationships then assumed an importance he never suspected earlier when he believed that the age of great revolutions was at an end and that he was living in the era of equality — according to his conception, a post-revolutionary epoch. The idea took root in his mind "more and more that we were making strides towards a fresh revolution" (9).

Like Marx, Tocqueville saw that the July Monarchy was the government of a class; that "all business was discussed among members of one class, in the interest and in the spirit of that class . . ." (8). Tocqueville now perceived the growing cleavage between what he called the upper and lower zones of French society: the upper in which some had hoped to confine all political life, but which was characterized by "languor, impotence, stagnation, and boredom"; and the lower in which "political life began to make itself manifest by means of feverish and irregular signs, of which the attentive observer was easily able to seize the meaning" (9).

Tocqueville tried to clarify that meaning in a document he drew up at the request of friends for a parliamentary session, but which never was published in his lifetime. The document was written in late 1847 (at about the same time Marx and Engels had drawn up their famous analysis and program in the form of a manifesto) not for the working class, of course, but rather for his colleagues in the dominant class and

ville and Democracy" in F. J. C. Hearnshaw, ed., *The Social and Political Ideas of Some Representative Thinkers of the Victorian Age* (London: Harrap, 1935), pp. 113–114; George Wilson Pierson, *Tocqueville and Beaumont in America* (New York: Oxford, 1938), p. 768; Edward T. Gargan, *Alexis de Tocqueville: The Critical Years 1848–1851* (Washington, D.C.: The Catholic University of America Press, 1955), pp. 251ff.; J. P. Mayer, *Alexis de Tocqueville* (New York: Viking, 1940), *passim.*, but especially 175 ff.; Raymond Aron, *Main Currents in Sociological Thought,* vol. I (London: Weidenfeld and Nicolson, 1968); and, finally, George Rudé's Introduction to Georges Duveau's *1848: The Making of a Revolution,* translated by Anne Carter (New York: Random House, 1968). The reader who feels himself relatively unfamiliar with the main historical events and actors of 1848 might profitably consult Duveau's fine study.

ruling elite. He warned them about the coming crisis: it would be a confrontation between the upper and lower classes and more particularly between the bourgeoisie and the proletariat. The country would soon be divided "between two great parties."

Like Marx, Tocqueville saw that the one great privilege that had quite naturally survived the revolution of 1789 was private property. He sensed that this would be the main issue in the near future. "Let not the proprietors deceive themselves as to the strength of their position, nor think that the rights of property form an insurmountable barrier because they have not as yet been surmounted; for our times are unlike any others" (11). Previously, the rights of property were easily defended, or rather never attacked. But, continues Tocqueville:

> today, when the rights of property are nothing more than the last remnants of an overthrown aristocratic world; when they alone are left intact, isolated privileges amid the universal levelling of society; when they are no longer protected behind a number of still more controversible [sic] and odious rights, the case is altered, and they alone are left daily to resist the direct and unceasing shock of democratic opinion. . . . Before long, the political struggle will be restricted to those who have and those who have not; property will form the great field of battle; and the principal political questions will turn upon the more or less important modifications to be introduced into the right of property. We shall then have once more among us great public agitations and great political parties (11).

"Haves and have-nots" now has for Tocqueville a rather precise sociological meaning. Most often it refers to the bourgeoisie and proletariat whom he came to regard, as did Marx, as the two main classes or historical actors of the modern era.

In another speech, delivered on the eve of the revolution, Tocqueville was more "urgent and explicit." In reply to those who doubted the urgency of the situation, he pointed specifically to the working class and to its revolutionary consciousness, which called into question the very foundations of the existing society. The new ideas, questioning the justice and equitability of the existing social order, would "bring with them sooner or later . . . a most formidable revolution." The governing classes, Tocqueville was convinced, were "sleeping on a volcano" and when the revolution came and these classes lost their power, the effective reason will have been ". . . that they have become unworthy to retain it" (13).

In general, considering classes and the relationships among them now became for Tocqueville a most important analytical tool, as for example in the following historical proposition that he probably learned and took over from Guizot: "Our history from 1789 to 1830 has been . . . a struggle to the death between the *Ancien Régime* . . . and the New France led by the Middle Classes" (2). Like Marx, he viewed the regime of Louis Philippe, that of the Orleanist dynasty, as the rule of a class that now monopolized power:

> In 1830 the triumph of the middle class had been definite and so thorough that all political power, every franchise, every prerogative, and the whole government was confined and, as it were, heaped up within the narrow limits of this one class, to the statutory exclusion of all beneath them and the actual exclusion of all above. Not only did it thus rule society, but it may be said to have formed it. It entrenched itself in every vacant place, prodigiously augmented the number of places and accustomed itself to live almost as much upon the treasury as upon its own industry (2–3).

Marx's analysis differed in the explicit attention he gave to social stratification within the middle class, the economic bases of the various strata, and the respective political factions or parties representing them. The July Monarchy, for Marx, was the political régime primarily of one faction of the bourgeoisie, the financial aristocracy, not of the whole middle class and certainly not of the industrial bourgeoisie. The financial aristocracy made the laws and headed the state administration. "The July Monarchy," Marx wrote, "was nothing other than a joint-stock company for the exploitation of France's national wealth, the dividends of which were divided among ministers, Chambers, 240,000 voters and their adherents." [3] And Louis Philippe was the company's director. Tocqueville also discerned how the government had become a business enterprise "which conducts all its transactions with a view to the profits accruing to the shareholders" (3–4). Characteristically, he adds from his aristocratic standpoint that though Louis Philippe had come from the noblest of families, he soon acquired bourgeois attributes. "He was extremely polite, but . . . it was the politeness of a merchant rather than of a prince. He hardly appreciated literature or art, but he passionately loved industry" (4). In short, he had become the chief of the bourgeoisie and was himself "bourgeois." Thus Tocqueville also understood that the Orleanists represented a certain class interest and that the struggle between them and the Legitimists was more than merely dynastic.

Equally apparent to Tocqueville was the working-class or what he called the "Socialistic character of the new revolution." Reflecting on the

---

[3] Marx and Engels, *Selected Works*, pp. 130–131.

February revolution of 1848, he noted its "uniquely and exclusively popular character" and "the omnipotence it had given to the people properly so-called — that is to say, *the classes who work with their hands* — over all others. . . . [T]he lower orders had suddenly become the masters of Paris" (78, italics added).

Although Tocqueville and Marx were viewing events from ideological perspectives fundamentally opposed to each other, their analyses were very similar. Both thinkers agreed that in all previous revolutions in France the working class had been a participant but had neither led the revolutions nor lent them a distinctively proletarian character, which had been the case in 1789 and 1830. The latter revolution, wrote Tocqueville, "was effected by the people, but the middle class had stirred it up and led it, and secured the principal fruits of it. The Revolution of February, on the contrary, seemed to be made entirely outside the *bourgeoisie* and against it" (78). The people, or more precisely the workers, now seemed "in sole possession of power." And Tocqueville now suspected that unlike the popular revolutions of the more remote past, for instance, those of Florence toward the close of the Middle Ages that resulted from "transient and special causes," the present upheaval "was brought about by causes very permanent and of a kind so general that, after stirring up France, it was to be expected that it would excite all the rest of Europe" (79). To Tocqueville, as indeed to Marx too for a while, it had appeared that the proletariat would rule Paris and even the nation, because, in Tocqueville's words, "thanks to centralization, he who reigns in Paris governs France" (79). In this regard both thinkers erred. They overestimated the power of the Parisian workers who were isolated from the rest of France, particularly the peasantry, the only other class that could have become their effective ally.

For Tocqueville, it was primarily the socialistic theories that had kindled the passions of the revolution, itself the logical and inevitable result of the long struggle for equality. His conception of poverty, as we have already seen in other contexts, was primarily relative and social-psychological; the people's condition had improved, he believed, but so had their expectations risen and their power increased. The poor and the humble had for sixty years dreamt of "issuing from their poverty and inferiority by means of their power," and had worked toward that end. When they saw that changing political institutions in no way improved their lot, or improved it "with a slowness quite incompatible" with their desires, they inevitably turned their attention from the merely political and attacked "the unalterable laws that constitute society itself"

(84). The people now challenged the right of private property that Tocqueville regarded as the very "foundation of our social order." For Tocqueville the ideas expressing these demands, "socialism," were alternatively either "monstrous," "grotesque," "ludicrous," or "mad."

In part, Tocqueville uses "socialism" to stigmatize as "mad" the notions of those who challenged the prevailing order at its foundation, private property. Socialism had three main characteristics all of which he despised. First, it appealed to the material passions of men, insisting that work should be enjoyable as well as useful while need rather than merit should constitute the criterion for reward. Second, it attacked private property, as illustrated in Proudhon's phrase, "Property is theft." Finally, it was a new form of slavery in which the state would become the master, tutor, and pedagogue of every man.[4] But he also used the term to oppose the mildest reforms, such as the right to work and organize—which was probably all the workers really wanted at the time. As a member of the Constitutional Committee he resolutely opposed including a clause affirming the principle of the *droit au travail*. Extending the social responsibilities of the state, he believed, would hasten the very development he feared, an omnipotent and omnipresent Leviathan.[5]

Marx's observations about the temper of the dominant classes at the time may fittingly be applied to Tocqueville. "Socialism!" Marx remarks ironically. "Even bourgeois liberalism is declared *Socialistic,* bourgeois enlightenment socialistic, bourgeois financial reform socialistic." [6] On the other hand, branding all reforms as "socialistic" was more than a mere demagogical political tactic. It signified that the bourgeoisie understood that all the weapons it had used to fell the feudal order could now be used against itself. Again in Marx's words, "It understood that all the so-called bourgeois liberties and organs of progress attacked and menaced its *class rule* at its social foundation and its political summit simultaneously, and had therefore become "socialistic!" The bourgeoisie did not realize, however, that it had no monopoly on the demagogic use of the term "socialist." Referring to the reaction to the revolution culminating in the coup of Louis Napoleon, Marx continues: "What the bourgeoisie did not grasp was the logical conclusion that its *own parliamentary régime,* that its *political rule* in general, was now also bound to meet with

---

[4] *Oeuvres Complètes,* ed. Gustave de Beaumont, 9 vols. (Paris: Michel Lévy, 1864–1875), vol. IX, pp. 536–552.

[5] See Gargan, *op. cit.,* pp. 96ff.

[6] Marx and Engels, *op. cit.,* p. 260.

the general verdict of condemnation as being *socialistic*." [7] We shall return to this point later.

Although their evaluations of the process differed, both Tocqueville and Marx saw a permanent thrust from below. Marx perceived the growing revolutionary consciousness of the working class and recognized that this consciousness was not the result of working-class efforts alone. The workers had participated as an ally of the bourgeoisie in all revolutions since 1789, for interests not primarily their own. They had again and again been used by the various bourgeois strata who, as soon as they had accomplished their aims, always more limited than those of the workers, discarded the latter and even turned against them. Every revolution won with the participation of the workers ended with their defeat — which happened most dramatically in June of 1848. Tocqueville also perceived this pattern but was delighted that the workers had been held in check and defeated. What Marx called the growing revolutionary class consciousness of the workers, which he welcomed, Tocqueville conceived as the alarming growth of "mad" ideas, which he feared and detested. It was always these ideas and passions, not their real privations, that accounted primarily for the workers' restlessness and revolt.

Although Tocqueville took a clear and unequivocal public stand against the workers and the revolution, he did express some ambivalence about revolution in general in his private memoirs, never published in his lifetime. Reflecting on the events of 1848 a few years afterward, he suggests that the laws governing the basic structure of society "will in the long run undergo modification; they have already done so in many of their principal parts. But will they ever be destroyed and replaced by others? It seems to me impracticable" (85). But he was not sure:

> the more I study the former condition of the world and see the world of our own day in greater detail, the more I consider the prodigious variety to be met with not only in laws, but in principles of law, and the different forms even now taken and retained, whatever one may say, by the rights of property on this earth—*the more I am tempted to believe that what we call necessary institutions are often no more than institutions to which we have grown accustomed, and that in matters of social constitution the field of possibilities is much more extensive than men living in these various societies are ready to imagine* (85, italics added).

---

[7] *Ibid.*, p. 261.

Tocqueville always remained fearful, however, of testing this proposition in practice.

THE APPEAL TO THE PEOPLE

Tocqueville's fear of the people is reflected in his opposition to the banquet scheme of his colleagues, Odilon Barrot and the other leaders of the dynastic opposition — a scheme designed to involve the people in antigovernment demonstrations. As his colleagues were now seeking support outside the middle classes for the first time in eighteen years, failure to arouse the people, he believed, would only weaken the opposition and strengthen the government. More important, however, was Tocqueville's fear that by appealing to the people one was opening a Pandora's box. For if "you succeed in rousing the people," he warned his friends, "you are no more able than I to foresee whither an agitation of this kind will lead you" (18).

And Tocqueville goes on to relate how, in fact, contrary to his initial expectations, the enthusiasm in the country for the banquets surpassed "not only the hopes, but the wishes of those who started [them]"; and how the government goaded the opposition into planning a banquet even in Paris, where originally one had not been planned, so that in effect the government and the opposition irritated, spurred, and "dragged each other towards the common abyss which neither of them as yet perceived" (19). The opposition insisted on its constitutional right of assembly and, therefore, of holding the banquets as planned, although the government maintained that under the laws of 1790 and 1791 it was empowered to prevent any public meeting that seemed to threaten the public peace. The spokesman also used the phrase "blind or hostile passions," referring presumably to the participation of the people, and said the government would never give in to them and would oppose by force the demonstrations in the guise of banquets. Tocqueville recorded that the Radical Chiefs, as he called them, also apparently feared awakening the people, being uncertain they could control them, so that the revolution ironically "was brought about and almost longed for by the men whom it eventually precipitated from power, and that it was only foreseen and feared by those who were to triumph by its means" (22).

In general, one sees in these private memoirs that Tocqueville's analysis *qua* analysis was in many respects similar to that of Marx in his *Class Struggles in France 1848–1850* and the *Eighteenth Brumaire of Louis Bonaparte*. Both thinkers were concerned with a wide range of complex circumstances leading to the revolution. Just as Marx's essays display an emphasis on general economic and political conditions but no dogmatic commitment to any single-cause theory, Tocqueville's analysis is concerned with various factors but also with general economic conditions. Marx could have subscribed completely to the following methodological remark by Tocqueville: "For my part, I detest . . . absolute systems, which represent all the events of history as dependent upon great first causes linked by the chain of fatality, and which, as it were, suppress men from the history of the human race" (68). Tocqueville, on the other hand, ascribed considerable importance to the changing economic conditions as a general cause of the revolution — although, as we shall see, this statement requires certain important qualifications. What were the main conditions that had led, in Tocqueville's view, to the revolutions of 1848? Of fundamental importance was the industrial revolution that during the preceding thirty years had transformed Paris into a principal manufacturing city of France, which led to the concentration of a large working-class population in that city, and to poverty and discontent, especially in times of economic depression. But the revolutionary discontent itself, Tocqueville repeatedly emphasizes, had to be attributed mainly to what he called "the disease of envy" permeating all strata of the society — the disease that expressed itself obviously and directly in the new economic and political theories that were constantly gaining headway. These "strove to prove that human misery was the work of laws and not of Providence, and that poverty could be suppressed by changing the conditions of society" (69) — a proposition whose validity Tocqueville continued to deny all his life. The final contributing condition was the great social instability of France since 1789 and the accompanying revolutionary tradition, or in Tocqueville's words ". . . the fluctuating state of society which had, in less than sixty years, undergone the shock of seven great revolutions . . ." (69).

Tocqueville and Marx concurred in their respective assessments of the revolutionaries of 1848 who, unlike those of 1789, offered nothing to the great mass of the people — the peasantry — without whose support significant revolutionary gains were impossible. Both thinkers observed that the revolutionary leaders did not know how to win to the side of the workers that great potential ally; they did not know how to use universal suffrage to obtain an assembly representative of the people; nor did they know how to act boldly by seizing power. Tocqueville's sharp analysis shows how precisely the political program of the revolutionary leaders alienated the peasants from the workers instead of winning them over. He writes:

> In establishing universal suffrage they [the revolutionaries] thought they were summoning the people to the assistance of the Revolution: they were only giving them arms against it. Nevertheless, I am far from believing that it was impossible to arouse revolutionary passions, even in the country districts. In France, every agriculturist owns some portion of the soil, and most of them are more or less involved in debt; it was not, therefore, the landlords that should have been attacked, but the creditors; not the abolition promised of the rights of property, but the abolition of debts. The demagogues of 1848 did not think of this scheme (112–113).

Similarly, Marx also recognized how the republic had announced itself to the peasant with a new tax, thus raising a barrier between peasants and workers; [8] and observed, too, how the form of servitude had changed in the French countryside:

> in the course of the nineteenth century the feudal lords were replaced by urban usurers; the feudal obligation that went with the land was replaced by the mortgage; aristocratic landed property was replaced by bourgeois capital. The small holding of the peasant is now only the pretext that allows the capitalist to draw profits, interest and rent from the soil, while leaving it to the tiller of the soil himself to see how he can extract his wages.[9]

Of course, Marx and Tocqueville criticize the republic and its leaders from opposing value standpoints: Marx would have wanted them to be more astute while Tocqueville was pleased that revolutionaries have seldom been "more stupid" (111). Indeed, eventually Tocqueville found himself at the barricades, quite literally, directing the struggle against the workers.

However, even on the analytical level, the respective views of the two thinkers profoundly differed. Tocqueville tended to make light of the privations of the industrial workers and the effects of the economic crisis upon them. "The crisis from which the workmen in large manufactures were suffering," he wrote to Nassau Senior soon after the February revolution, "lasted a very short time, and though severe was not unexampled. It was not want, but ideas, that brought about that violent Subversion; chimerical ideas on the relations between labour and capital, extravagant theories as to the degree in which government might interfere between

---

[8] *Ibid.*, p. 141.

[9] *Ibid.*, p. 305.

working man and employer. . . . I repeat, we have to contend with ideas rather than with wants." [10] And because ideas, and not real human want or need, were at the root of the revolution, the main point was to overthrow the men of 1848 with their "mad follies" and "false systems" — without, however, destroying the republic, if possible.

THE JUNE DAYS

If before 1848 Tocqueville had believed that the age of great revolutions was over, now he could not be sure. It now appeared that all the revolutionary upheavals since 1789 were phases of one continuous, permanent revolution (73). His conception of historical developments now roughly approximated that of Marx.

Already by 1789, but increasingly thereafter, the economic development of France, particularly Paris, made it unavoidable that the working class should not only participate in each revolution but also try to lend it a proletarian character. Although the proletariat was the rear guard of the bourgeoisie and was used by that class for its own purposes, the workers nevertheless raised their voices during each revolutionary outbreak, making distinctive demands related to their own class interests. To be sure, these interests were not always clear and the demands differed according to the various groups and strata within the working class. Unclear and confused though the demands were, nonetheless both Marx and Tocqueville regarded them as elements of a new consciousness, which found its most explicit expression in the various currents of socialism. Marx, of course, regarded proletarian class consciousness as a potentially liberating force that, as it achieved ever greater clarity, would result in a movement to abolish private property, class cleavages, and class antagonisms. Tocqueville, on the other hand, viewed socialism as a mad and dangerous system of ideas that had to be overthrown.

Although working-class participation was somewhat evident in the pre-1848 revolutions, it became especially pronounced in 1848, when the workers not only put forward their demands more clearly than ever before, they did so arms in hand. And when those bourgeois factions and the other members of the opposition who wanted to enlarge the so-called "legal country" had achieved this limited objective, they turned upon their erstwhile allies, the workers, as the major menace.

To understand how the June days came about one has to go back to

---

[10] *Correspondence and Conversations of Alexis de Tocqueville with Nassau Senior*, vol. I (London: Henry S. King, 1872), pp. 35–36.

the "banquet" affair. The banquets had been sponsored and planned by the dynastic opposition to mobilize the classes "below," thereby increasing pressure upon the July Monarchy to reform and enlarge the franchise. This, then, was the limited goal of the opposition but events got out of hand, as Tocqueville had feared and foreseen. When the crisis erupted between the government and the opposition, the workers took to the streets. The monarchy soon fell, Louis Philippe fled, and the workers and their leaders believed they had contributed not only to establishing a republic but to what they called a "social" republic.

Both Tocqueville and Marx saw clearly that no one, not even the workers themselves, knew precisely what they meant by a "social" republic. But they held power and controlled Paris. As long as the workers had stood with the parties of the bourgeois opposition, and as long as they had fought as its rear guard and had thus ensured its victory, the proletariat was a dangerous but useful ally and hence tolerated. Now, however, that the workers were standing arms in hand apparently against the bourgeoisie, i.e., attending to their own interests and making their own demands, they had become the main enemy and had to be disarmed. The new bourgeois government provoked the confrontation by attempting to rid Paris of the unemployed workers. This led directly to the June uprising that Tocqueville and Marx described in much the same terms.

On June 21, 1848, the *Moniteur* published the decree ordering the expulsion of all unmarried workers from the national *ateliers* or their conscription into the army. Marx wrote:

> The workers were left no choice, they had to starve or let fly. They answered on June 22 with the tremendous insurrection in which the first great battle was fought between the two classes that split modern society. It was a fight for the preservation or annihilation of the bourgeois order. The veil that shrouded the republic was torn asunder.
>
> It is well known how the workers, with unexampled bravery and ingenuity, without leaders, without a common plan, without means and, for the most part, lacking weapons, held in check for five days the army, the Mobile Guard, the Paris National Guard, and the National Guard that streamed in from the provinces. It is well known how the bourgeoisie compensated itself for the mortal anguish it suffered by unheard-of brutality, massacring over 3,000 prisoners.[11]

Tocqueville's view coincides rather strikingly. "As we know," he wrote, "it was the closing of the national workshops that occasioned the rising"

---

[11] Marx and Engels, *op. cit.*, p. 147.

(161). And like Marx he notes the bravery and skill of the workers: ". . . the insurgents fought without a war-cry, without leaders, without flags, and yet with a marvelous harmony and amount of military experience that astonished the oldest officers" (160). Tocqueville also agreed that what appeared to be *the* distinguishing feature of the June revolution as compared with all preceding ones was "that it did not aim at changing the form of government but at altering the order of society" (160). It was "a struggle of class against class, a sort of Servile war" (160). And he adds, finally: "It must also be observed that this formidable insurrection was not the enterprise of a certain number of conspirators, but the revolt of one whole section of the population against another" (161).

Both thinkers agreed that the workers rose in part as a result of their exposure to revolutionary theories. For Tocqueville, however, these theories were totally false:

> We behold in it [socialism] nothing more than a blind and rude, but powerful, effort on the part of the workmen to escape from the necessities of their condition, which had been depicted to them as one of unlawful oppression, and to open up by main force a road towards that imaginary comfort with which they had been deluded. It was this mixture of greed and false theory which first gave birth to the insurrection and then made it so formidable. These poor people had been told that the wealth of the rich was in some way the produce of a theft practised upon themselves. They had been assured that the inequality of fortunes was as opposed to morality and the welfare of society as it was to nature. Prompted by their needs and their passions, many had believed this obscure and erroneous notion of right, which, mingled with brute force, imparted to the latter an energy, a tenacity and a power which it would never have possessed unaided (160–161).

Although Tocqueville here acknowledges that the workers were prompted by needs as well as passions, he insists that mainly "false theory" had impelled the workers to act. He now denies all validity to the theory that asserts that social conditions and institutions may be changed. Had he not himself earlier acknowledged that what often appears as a necessary institution may only be one to which men have grown accustomed? Then why maintain that a false theory teaches men that what has appeared as the "necessities of their condition" may not be necessary at all? And why so strong a reaction against the workers—especially since he saw clearly how the great battle was provoked and that the workers wanted only to assure themselves of the right to work, the only dignified means of subsistence they had. Here we see rather clearly Tocque-ville's social and political standpoint. His occasional ambivalence not-withstanding, he thought and acted as a dedicated member of the ruling elite to which he belonged. He professed to despise the "iron laws" and fatalistic character of certain philosophical systems, and in theory he attributed to men the ability, however small, to make history. Yet the morality and consciousness he wished to impose on the lower classes was submission and resignation to the so-called "necessities of their condition."

Marx regarded the June events as a terrible tragedy but only a tempo-rary defeat. "The revolution is dead! — Long live the revolution!" he exclaimed. Because the *basic structure of society had remained intact,* the probability was great that it would continue to generate discontent, rebellion, and resistance. Tocqueville agreed that the revolution was only temporarily dead, but characteristically his emphasis is fundamen-tally different:

> Such were the days of June, necessary and disastrous days. They did not extinguish revolutionary ardour in France, but they put a stop, at least for a time, to what may be called the work appertaining to the Revolution of February. They delivered the nation from the tyranny of the Paris workmen and restored it to possession of itself.
>
> Socialistic theories continued to penetrate into the minds of the people in the shape of envious and greedy desires, and to sow the seed of future revolutions . . . (196–197).

Tocqueville's later reflections about socialism make it altogether evi-dent that he recognized that the reaction following the revolution would destroy not only "socialism" but liberalism as well. Yet, the workers had to be put down, he continues to insist. He had seen rather clearly that all who entered the lists against them, himself included, were contribut-ing to the process that would soon threaten the basic liberties of all. Nevertheless, he pursued the same policy relentlessly.[12]

---

12 The judgment of a devoted and sympathetic Tocqueville scholar in this regard is that by supporting and fashioning the policy that resolutely and con-sistently rejected even the mildest and most rudimentary demands of the workers: "Tocqueville must share some of the responsibility for the destruction of the Republic which he believed himself dedicated to preserve. Tocqueville's respon-sibility is more direct than that of others because he understood fully that the social character of the Revolution could not be drawn off from its current." See Gargan, *op. cit.*, pp. 89–90, which is probably the most comprehensive study of Tocqueville's thought and action during the crucial years of 1848–1851.

In the period immediately following the revolutions of 1848 Tocqueville and his colleagues had as their aim the maintenance of the weakened republic "by governing it in a regular, moderate, conservative and absolutely constitutional way . . ." (228). Tocqueville did not believe, however, that the republican form was best for France. A republic, whose main characteristic he now saw as the "executive power," was in France extremely vulnerable: "its instability will always be, in periods of excitement, a cause of revolution, and, in peaceful times, a cause of great uneasiness. Moreover, I have always considered the Republic an ill-balanced form of government, which always promised more, but gave less, liberty than the Constitutional Monarchy" (238). He was again looking wistfully across the channel, but realized that the English model was not a real option for France.

Monarchy, even in its constitutional form, meant at least partially restoring the old order, which would be impossible both because the old dynasty "was profoundly antipathetic to the majority of the country" and because "the one genuine passion that remained alive in France" was hatred of the old regime. And after the experience with Louis Philippe and the Orleanists, the people were anything but favorably inclined toward them. As for Louis Napoleon, Tocqueville sensed that he might replace the republic. Indeed, he already held power, having been elected primarily by the peasantry in December 1848, "But what would come of his success," Tocqueville muses, "except a bastard Monarchy, despised by the enlightened classes, hostile to liberty, governed by intriguers, adventurers, and valets?" Having thus foreseen rather clearly what one might today call the proto-fascistic nature of Louis Bonaparte's regime, Tocqueville nonetheless adds, characteristically: "Not one of these results would justify a new revolution" (239).

Under these circumstances, Tocqueville believed that maintaining the republic would be extremely difficult. The upper classes, who were fit to govern, detested the republic. That they should rule or at least dominate such a government he considered both necessary and desirable; but he also understood that this would probably generate great discontent among the people. On the other hand, it had become obvious that the middle classes could not rule by themselves, but required the support of the lower classes — a prospect altogether unacceptable to Tocqueville and his colleagues. What remained then as the strongest possibility in the immediate future was the "bastard monarchy" of Louis Bonaparte, who had the following of what Tocqueville called the "footman class" and of what Marx called the *Lumpenproletariat*. This appeared to Tocqueville as very likely because he correctly foresaw how any new crisis, domestic or foreign, would strengthen Bonaparte's hand. Indeed, what he expected and feared soon occurred.

Tocqueville, who by now had accepted a cabinet position for both personal and patriotic considerations, learned upon entering it that three days earlier the government of Louis Bonaparte had given orders to the army to attack Rome — or more precisely the republican and revolutionary forces in Rome — despite the fact that the Constituent Assembly had just passed a resolution explicitly prohibiting the government from doing so. Tocqueville writes: "This flagrant disobedience of the injunctions of a sovereign assembly, this war undertaken against a people in revolution, because of its revolution, and in defiance of the terms of the Constitution which commanded us to respect all foreign nationalities, made inevitable and brought nearer the conflict which we dreaded" (244).

Here one sees still another instance of Tocqueville's occasional ambivalence and how he resolved it. He decried the "flagrant" violation of the Constitution. Yet, when the Mountain, in the person of Ledru-Rollin, challenged the government, Tocqueville refused even to show him the relevant documents. The violation of the Constitution meant a further weakening of constitutional government and a further strengthening of the executive power. But now this evil was the lesser by far (despite Tocqueville's frequently repeated commitment to constitutional government), compared with the apparent threat of "civil war" — Ledru-Rollin had threatened that "the republicans will know how to command respect for the constitution by every means, be it even by force of arms." Tocqueville refused to support the motion for the impeachment of Bonaparte that Ledru-Rollin had laid on the president's table. To support such a motion was inconceivable, especially as it had originated from "below."

Actually, Tocqueville disapproved not so much the purpose of the expedition to Rome as the way it "had been undertaken and conducted." And eventually he worked for the restoration of Pius IX, but argued that the restored pope should be "liberal and lenient" (333). What he wanted, however, was a limited liberty, a liberty of a certain kind. In a speech on the Roman expedition delivered to the National Legislative Assembly in his role as Foreign Minister, Tocqueville quite candidly reported that:

> in our negotiations with the Pope we did not press for the grant of institutions which might immediately establish great political liberty. We

refrained from doing so because recent history and our own experiences had taught us that in the state in which the Roman people are at present, faced as they are with a moderate liberal party disorganized and terrified, an anarchical party full of folly and fury and an inert mass, it would have been unwise to ask the Holy Father too insistently to restore the institutions which had already led to his overthrow. Therefore, we did not press, I say again, for institutions conferring great political liberty (334).

When the *Motu Proprio* was issued by the restored Pius IX, it promised reforms but specified none in particular; and although Tocqueville acknowledged that the document "had not fully realized our expectations," he emphasized the hostility of the old regime in Rome even to the general reforms promised, and remained satisfied with the document and the hopes it held out.

The civil war he had feared never materialized — although sporadic fighting in the provinces had lasted a few hours. What one saw in Paris on June 13, 1849, was a peaceful demonstration. Some 30,000 followers of the *Montaigne,* moving along with the cry "Long live the Constitution!" were very soon dispersed by troops with fixed bayonets. As the historian Emile Bourgeois later observed, the demonstration provided "an excellent pretext to decimate the Democratic party by means of severe measures — arrests in Paris and in the provinces, prosecutions and a state of seige. Banquets were forbidden, mutual benefit societies dissolved, and Republican school-teachers suspended or arbitrarily dismissed." [13] In short, a great repressive wave was turned not only against the workers but above all against the middle class. The constitution had now become, in Thiers' words, "a dirty piece of paper." Tocqueville himself supported the siege as well as the repressive measures against the clubs and the press; [14] to save liberty, he argued, it was now necessary to restrict it(261).

With the constitution largely destroyed Tocqueville suspected that salvaging what he called a "moderate republic" would be more difficult than ever. The Montagnards, whom he somehow classified with the antirepublican forces, were more dangerous in their defeat than before, because they bore great ill-will against those who had so severely

---

[13] *The Cambridge Modern History* (Cambridge: Cambridge University Press, 1909), vol. XI, p. 126.

[14] As Gargan correctly observes, Tocqueville's support "cannot be explained by his theoretical position towards a free society. It is explained by examining the political realism with which he accepted office in a Ministry that he hoped would be dominated by those of his political convictions." *Op. cit.*, p. 137.

repressed them. The parliamentary majority, excluding the party of Louis Napoleon ("too few in number and of too evil repute to count"), consisted of "sixty to eighty" moderate republicans, the Legitimists, and the Orleanists. Of the two dynastic parties, the former, Tocqueville believed, was more likely to support the republic "for it had destroyed their destroyer, and had opened up to them the prospect of power . . ." (255). A handful of moderates, then, in coalition with the old dynastic party were to defend the republic from the recently defeated but still dangerous Montagnards and at the same time "hinder the establishment of the bastard Monarchy of Louis Napoleon. This was at the time the nearest threatening danger" (255).

To save the republic with "parties which do not love it" required that the coalition should retain its power, which, in turn, required great adroitness, especially the ability to compromise and make concessions. As usual, the concessions were to be made to the "Party of Order" but never to the other side. But the policy of the "Party of Order" in its struggle with the forces of "anarchy," a policy Tocqueville essentially endorsed, had significantly strengthened the executive and, therefore, Louis Bonaparte. Also, the more conservative members of the coalition were opportunistically using Tocqueville's more liberal group to legitimize the repression while at the same time conspiring with Bonaparte. "We were informed by our agents," wrote Tocqueville, "that most of them [the conservatives], but especially M. Thiers and M. Molé, were constantly seeing him in private, and urging him with all their might to overthrow, in concert with them, and at their common expense and to their common profit, the Republic" (266). Tocqueville observes that they were merely deluding themselves that "Louis Napoleon was still happy in their leading-strings," because he had his own plans and ambitions and "endured their yoke with great impatience." Under these circumstances, what appeared to Tocqueville as the best strategy was that he and his colleagues within the coalition should "remain independent of these great wire-pullers, and . . . uphold the Executive Power against their attacks" (267).

Tocqueville had hoped to satisfy Louis Napoleon's ambitions by promising him a revision of the constitution, particularly Article 45, which prohibited the reelection of the president. If efforts to revise failed, Tocqueville suggested to the president that he might be reelected "at the end of his term of office, in spite of Article 45, by an almost unanimous vote. . . ." In return, the president was to promise that he would govern France "peacefully, wisely, modestly, not aiming at more than being the first magistrate of the nation, and not its corrupter or its master . . ." (268). Tocqueville was prepared to make a deal with Louis Napoleon, whom he viewed, as did Marx, as a mediocrity raised to a high level by propitious circumstances, who surrounded himself with "gaol-birds," "intriguers and rascals." Tocqueville failed to see that the president already had learned, in December 1848, how much charisma he had inherited from his celebrated uncle. Louis Bonaparte could appeal directly to the people and therefore had no need for Tocqueville and his colleagues.[15]

Although he was eventually to win, Louis Bonaparte temporarily had overestimated his strength. On March 10, 1850, by-elections were held to fill the vacant seats formerly occupied by representatives who, because of the repression, were now either in prison or in exile. The results astounded many, especially the president and the party of order, including Tocqueville. "The Republican list," wrote the historian Emile Bourgeois, "with men like Carnot, Vidal, and De Flotte, was carried by a majority of a thousand votes over the list from the Rue de Poitiers supported by Louis Napoleon. In the provinces, eighteen Republicans were elected out of twenty-eight." This victory at the polls "was due to the final completion and cementing of the union between Moderates, Radicals, and Socialists which was effected once a dictatorship seemed imminent and a clerical reaction to be feared." [16] Now both Napoleon and the Party of Order saw their power threatened once again — this time not by civil war or "anarchy" but by the people's will expressed at the ballot-box.

Commenting on the elections, Marx wrote:

Paris elected only social-democratic candidates. It even concentrated most of the votes on the insurgent of June 1848, on DeFlotte. Thus did the

---

[15] Gargan observes that when Tocqueville offered his proposition to Louis Napoleon, the latter had been in office only eight months, thus leaving at least two years until the problem of reelection would arise. "It must, therefore, have been a source of satisfaction to Louis Napoleon to have Alexis de Tocqueville, a professed devotee of political purity, hurrying to him with his nervous promises. Without solicitation he offered much and threatened only the withdrawal of his personal support if the President acted in an unseemly manner." *Op. cit.*, p. 75. Therefore, Tocqueville's action, in the name of political realism, may have betrayed just how feeble was the resistance he was prepared to offer Bonaparte and how few obstacles he was actually able to place in his path. Instead of containing Bonaparte's ambitions, as Tocqueville had hoped, he may very well have contributed to them.

[16] Emile Bourgeois, article in *The Cambridge Modern History* (Cambridge: Cambridge University Press, 1909), vol. XI, p. 131.

Parisian petty bourgeoisie, in alliance with the proletariat, revenge itself for its defeat on June 13, 1849. . . . One circumstance seemed to heighten the peril of this election victory. The army voted in Paris for the June insurgent against La Hitte, a minister of Bonaparte's and in the Departments largely for the Montagnards who here, too, though indeed not so decisively as in Paris, maintained the ascendancy over their adversaries.

Bonaparte saw himself suddenly confronted with revolution once more. . . . [H]e disappeared behind the Party of Order.[17]

Marx goes on to observe that though Bonaparte's position was now seriously weakened, "The Party of Order proved unable to take advantage of this opportunity that would never return." [18] Even then Tocqueville and his liberal colleagues systematically excluded from their political calculations the only forces really interested in and capable of preserving the republic.

Moreover, on May 8 the parliamentary majority introduced a law effectively abolishing universal suffrage. As a result of the law, almost three million citizens "were deprived of their political rights on the pretext that they had not resided three years in one place, and were consequently 'vagabonds,' or 'anarchists' and 'criminals,' if they had taken part in a club or secret society, or if they had been convicted before a political tribunal. Shortly afterwards clubs and public meetings even for election purposes were forbidden, for the future, by the Act of June 9, 1850." [19] Emile Bourgeois' description of the ensuing proto-fascistic situation deserves to be quoted in full:

Following on these enactments a regular reign of terror and persecution was deliberately inaugurated against the Republican party throughout France. The Administration of Justice under Rouher cooperated with the Executive under Baroche. House to house distribution of books or pamphlets, meetings and banquets, in any form, were forbidden. The Republican representatives of the nation were reduced to receiving their constituents one at a time in cafés watched by the police. Any gathering of people who might talk politics was eyed with suspicion by gendarmes, magistrates, and prefects. The houses of Republicans were searched daily. The smallest societies where Republicans met were . . . broken up as secret societies. The Republican newspapers were hunted down and overwhelmed with lawsuits and fines. Officials, postmen, surveyors of roads, and school-teachers were

---

[17] Marx and Engels, *op. cit.*, vol. I, p. 262.
[18] *Ibid.*, p. 263.
[19] Bourgeois, *op. cit.*, p. 132.

dismissed on the slightest suspicion. Mayors, officers of the National Guard, and municipal councillors suffered a like fate so soon as information had been given against them. The cry of "Vive la République" became an act of sedition, that of "Vive Napoléon" was commended and rewarded. Absurd as it may seem even the wearing of red in belts, ties, or caps, became actionable.[20]

By 1851, Napoleon's victory seemed assured and the only real question was whether it would be by "legitimate" means or by force. Napoleon preferred "peaceful" means, having terrorized and intimidated large sections of the populace, and tried such means first. Approaching Odilon Barrot, Malleville, Tocqueville, and others, he persuaded them to "endeavour to extort from the Assembly a vote approving the prolongation of his tenure of office."[21] Tocqueville favored ·and worked for this prolongation, which the Republicans opposed as a "legalized" dictatorship. The project was defeated by nearly 100 votes.

Thwarted by the assembly, Napoleon now decided to strike. On the night of December 12, 1851, he decided to dissolve the assembly, issuing at the same time a proclamation restoring universal suffrage and informing the people of a plebiscite on the revision of the constitution. The proclamation was accompanied by the full force of the state. This time, however not only Socialists and Republicans were incarcerated, repressed, or terrorized, but all who had opposed the revision of the constitution for whatever reason, "whether in the interests of crown or people."[22] On December 21, 1851, he won the plebiscite, i.e., the right to alter the constitution as he wished. Less than a year later, the "parody" that had begun in February 1848 was complete: "the hereditary Empire in the person of Napoleon III" was restored.[23]

Tocqueville had foreseen much of this development. He also understood that basically the only effective way to forestall it was to turn to the people — an option he so much feared that it always remained unthinkable. Even when he clearly perceived that the reaction to the revolution was destroying liberalism as well as radical republicanism and

---

[20] *Ibid.*, p. 132.

[21] *Ibid.*, p. 133.

[22] *Ibid.*, p. 136. Tocqueville, as reporter for two hundred and thirty other protesting deputies, made a token protest in the form of a letter to the English *Times* and received a token punishment: twenty-four hours' imprisonment in the barracks of the Quai d'Orsay.

[23] *Ibid.*, p. 141.

socialism, he maintained the same position. A few months before the coup d'état, he wrote to Nassau Senior:

> I believe that the Bonapartist current, if it can be turned aside at all, can be turned aside only by meeting a revolutionary current, which will be still more dangerous. . . .
>
> The government which I should prefer, if I thought it possible, would be a republic; but, believing its continuance impossible, I should see without regret Louis Napoleon become our permanent ruler, if I could believe that he would be supported by the higher classes, and would be able and desirous to rule constitutionally. But . . . I [do] not believe either of these things to be possible. . . .
>
> His reelection, therefore, especially if illegal, may have disastrous consequences. And yet it is inevitable, unless resisted by an appeal to revolutionary passions, which I do not wish to rouse in the nation.[24]

Clearly, Tocqueville recognized that there was indeed a way of preventing the new Caesarism. If he systematically shunned anything that remotely resembled an appeal to the people, it was because he thought and acted as a dedicated member of the ruling elite. It was precisely as such that he believed the people would be "more dangerous" than Bonaparte's despotism — more dangerous to the privileged classes, that is.

The substance of Tocqueville's social and moral outlook becomes altogether evident in his *Souvenirs,* particularly in his perception of the lower classes and in his use of the term "socialist." A "socialist" was not one who subscribed to a social and political theory or doctrine but rather one who possessed certain psychological traits, character, and state of mind. During the June days, he had returned home one evening to learn that the house-porter, who was enthusiastic about the revolution, had threatened to kill him. Tocqueville describes the porter as ". . . a man of very bad reputation in the neighborhood, an old soldier, not quite in his right mind, a drunkard, and a great good-for-nothing, who spent at the wine-shop all the time which he did not employ in beating his wife. This man might be said to be a Socialist by birth, or rather by temperament" (184).

In the morning, Tocqueville's manservant, whom he had provided with a gun and a National Guard's uniform, and who presumably had been fighting the insurgents, arrived. The contrasting terms in which Tocqueville describes this man are significant: "This one was certainly not a

---

24 *Correspondence and Conversations of Alexis de Tocqueville with Nassau William Senior* (London: Henry S. King, 1872), vol. I, 264–266.

Socialist, either in theory or temperament. He was not even tainted in the slightest degree with the most general malady of the age, restlessness of mind, and even in other times than ours it would have been difficult to find a man more contented with his position and less sullen at his lot . . ." (186). Tocqueville then relates how his contented servant "took off his uniform, cleaned my boots, brushed my clothes, and putting on his uniform again [said]: 'If you don't require me any more sir, and if you will permit me, I will go back to the fighting.'" And Tocqueville recalls how ". . . I experienced a sort of reposeful feeling, during these days filled with turmoil and hate, when I looked at the young man's peaceful and contented face" (187). Tocqueville would have preferred that all the lowly and humble be like that young man: content in their lot and never falling prey to the "malady of the age, restlessness of mind."

For Tocqueville, poverty and the other troubles of the poor were not a condition in which people were deprived of real human needs. Poverty was rather a psychological phenomenon; the poor, ultimately, were among those who, as he had expressed himself years earlier, had received "from God the special and dangerous mission of providing for the material well-being of the rest of society." [25] As for industrial workers, Drescher has accurately summarized Tocqueville's view: "Permanent poverty and insecurity were . . . as providential and permanent for industrial workers as equalization was for the remainder of society." [26]

Nor, incidentally, did his "law" of providential equality and democracy apply to dependent peoples or colonies — particularly those of France. In a report on Algeria submitted to the Chamber of Deputies in 1847, Tocqueville wrote: "It is neither necessary nor useful to give our Moslem subjects exaggerated ideas of their own importance, nor to persuade them that we are obligated always to treat them precisely as if they were fellow citizens and equals." Domination of the colonies by force would be required "for a century, if not forever." [27] Clearly, certain categories of human beings were destined always to remain outside the so-called universal law he had enunciated in his *Democracy*.

---

[25] Quoted in Seymour Drescher, *Dilemmas of Democracy: Tocqueville and Modernization* (Pittsburgh: University of Pittsburgh Press, 1968), p. 108.
[26] *Ibid.*, p. 109.
[27] *Ibid.*, p. 194.

7. The Old Regime and the French Revolution

WITH THE COUP and the Second Empire Tocqueville's political career came to an end once and for all. He now turned once again from politics to scholarship, which was in any case more suited to his temperament and more likely, he sensed, to grant him the immortality he strongly craved. Soon after the coup he wrote to Beaumont: "I have thought a hundred times that if I am to leave any traces of myself in this world, it will be far more by what I shall have written than by what I shall have done." [1] His scholarship, however, remained *engagé*. His last great work was more than a study of the old order and the conditions that led to the upheaval of 1789; it was also a thinly veiled but feeble indictment of the Second Empire, as well as an inquiry into its origins.

To understand how the *Old Regime* became all these things at once, one must realize that after 1851 Tocqueville became again preoccupied with the political concentration of power in France, a problem that now loomed larger than ever before. His fear of, and interest in, the Parisian proletariat declined together with working-class unrest and the threat of working-class insurrection. It is apparent that even at this late date Tocqueville had not seen clearly that the capitalist-industrial system would play an increasingly important role in shaping the structure and process of modern society; nor had he fully recognized how much the events of 1848–1851 and the struggles accompanying the consolidation of that society had to do with the triumph of the dictatorship. Perhaps because of his own role in those events he could not, or would not, admit

---

[1] Quoted in Richard Herr, *Tocqueville and the Old Regime* (Princeton, N.J.: Princeton University Press, 1962), p. 18.

this either publicly or to himself, which, with his persistent *idée mère,* may explain why Tocqueville now turned to the more remote past where he sought the key to the process that resulted in the coup and the Second Empire.

The central idea of Tocqueville's final work, as of his early ones, is still the struggle between aristocracy and democracy, the destruction of the former and the ascendancy of the latter. After his recent political experiences, however, he now made the concept of social class a more important element of his analysis. More, class alienation and hostility had paved the way to both the revolution and the first empire. To be sure, twenty years earlier he had presented a similar analysis in his article on the old order.[2] At that time, however, he had placed the blame squarely on the ruling class, the nobility, whereas now he shifted responsibility, somewhat, to the central power and the kings — as if he wanted to absolve himself and the other members of his class by showing that the events that led to the despotism of his time had been predetermined long before he was born.[3]

In his *Old Regime* Tocqueville was now more sensitive to the fact that an adequate understanding of French history and society required a knowledge of "the exact relations that obtained among the various classes" (70). And in another passage, he pauses to remind his reader that: "Undoubtedly one could produce individuals as evidence against my generalization; however I am discussing classes which alone ought to concern the historian" (179). Now, in place of the rather ambiguous terms, "aristocracy" and "democracy," that had dominated his earlier works, one sees a reference to specific classes and the conflicts among them. The following exposition, then, emphasizes how important in Tocqueville's analytical framework the concept of class relations now became.[4]

---

[2] Alexis de Tocqueville, *Oeuvres Complètes,* Edition définitive publiée sous la direction de J. P. Mayer, tome II, part I, *L'Ancien Régime et la Révolution* (Paris: *Gallimard,* 1952–). This volume also contains the article "Etat Social et politique de la France avant et depuis 1789," pp. 33–66. References to *L'Ancien Régime* in this volume are hereafter indicated by the page number in parentheses immediately following the cited passage. Translations are mine.

[3] For a discussion of this point see Herr, *op. cit.,* especially pp. 80, 84, 112.

[4] For an exploration of Tocqueville's conceptions of class and class relations as they might apply to revolutions in general see Melvin Richter, "Tocqueville's Contributions to the Theory of Revolution," in *Revolution,* Nomos VIII, Carl J. Friedrich, ed. (New York: Atherton, 1966), pp. 75–121.

What appeared to Tocqueville as distinctive about the French Revolution was that, despite its political objectives, it had all the attributes of a religious revolution. It was, first of all, universal, or all-European; it transcended national boundaries and appealed to all men; it sought proselytes the world over and even spread a gospel. Indeed, much like Christianity, perhaps the first religious movement that cut across kinship and other parochial lines, the French Revolution taught the fraternity of all men. It appealed to them on the basis of abstract, universal principles and called for a regeneration of all humanity. Of course, political movements with a universal character had occurred before in history. It was not, therefore, the ideas and the methods of the French Revolution that were unprecedented, but rather their success. Its "great novelty," Tocqueville suggests, "is that so many peoples should have arrived to the point at which such methods could be effectively employed and such revolutionary maxims so readily accepted" (90). He understood very well that: "For doctrines of this kind to produce revolutions, it is necessary that certain changes should already have taken place in the living conditions, customs, and morals, which made men's minds more receptive to new ideas" (89). Thus, revolution had a universal appeal because almost all European nations shared the same institutions, which, however, were decomposing everywhere.

This generalization could be applied to all Europe though less to the east, where feudal institutions seemed more stable, than to the west. In western Europe Tocqueville singled out for comparative sociological discussion France, England, and Germany, whose feudal social structure had been quite similar. The same social, political-administrative principles had prevailed in all three countries: "Society was divided in the same manner and the same hierarchy was evident among the various classes; nobles occupied identical positions, and had the same appearances; this was so much the case that one might say they were not different men but the same men everywhere" (92). The decay of this structure, however, which began as early as the Middle Ages, left the old order everywhere "half in ruins" by the eighteenth century. What seemed beyond dispute was the progressive decline of aristocratic institutions and values; ironically, the weaker they became, the more they were detested. The institutions of the old order retained their original forms but were being drained of their substance. Most important, the nobles in the provincial assemblies were losing the allegiance of the people who were becoming more and more inclined to put their faith in the monarchy (93). Everyone, everywhere, it seemed, expressed a growing contempt for the old.

The causes of this historical process, however, Tocqueville leaves largely unexplored at this stage of his analysis. Although he seems to be on the border of the idea that there were new forces at work contributing to the dissolution of the old order, he never points to them precisely. He notes that the decay of the feudal institutions was accompanied "in Germany as well as in France by a steadily increasing prosperity." And he adds: "But what merits special attention is the fact that everything that was most vital, active, and productive was new, and not merely new but contrary to the past" (94). Specifically Tocqueville mentions only the new spirit now animating the royalty. A centralized state bureaucracy increasingly undermined the power of the nobility and replaced it in local government.

In his reference to England, however, he alludes directly to the class relations that made feudalism a dead letter by the seventeenth century. Already then one could observe in that country many new phenomena virtually unknown to the society of the Middle Ages: classes intermingling, the eclipse of the nobility, an open aristocracy, wealth as the basis of power, equality before the law, equality of access to public office, freedom of the press, and freedom of speech. In France, too, the old order had changed profoundly long before the revolution; with different results, however. Tocqueville is preparing to answer the question: What were the consequences of the French Revolution? In reply he will argue that the break with the past in 1789 was far less radical than was generally supposed.

The revolution was the violent culmination of a long historical process. In fact, it was not even a culmination because the revolution was permanent and continued in his own day. If the explosion of 1789 had never occurred, the old order would in any case have crumbled everywhere, but slowly instead of collapsing all at once. But if feudal conditions prevailed before the revolution throughout continental Europe, why were they apparently so much more detested in France?

If the main aim and effect of the revolution was to destroy feudalism, then why did it not break out elsewhere, for example, in those countries in which feudalism was a much heavier yoke? In Germany, for instance, serfdom, strictly speaking, was still in effect at the time of the revolution. The peasant was subject to many feudal constraints, including what the French called *corvée,* which "in certain districts compelled him to give not less than three days' labor a week" (99). In France, in contrast, these conditions had long since disappeared; "the peasant could come and go, buy and sell, enter into contracts and work as he pleased" (100). Serfdom had been abolished "in an epoch so remote that its very date had been forgotten." Moreover, the French peasant had early become something of a landowner. Splitting up the estates, Tocqueville argues against the commonly accepted view, was not the exclusive work of the revolution; much earlier there existed a comparatively large number of peasant proprietors. In this respect France was unique.

The records showed that in France a petit-bourgeois stratum of peasants already owned land and that it was they who bought the land of the Church and the nobility parcelled out during the revolution. So its main effect was not so much to divide the land nor to create a class of free proprietors, but rather to transfer the land from feudal to bourgeois hands, to the small bourgeois proprietors who now, however, "were greatly impeded in the exploitation of the land as they shouldered numerous charges and imposts from which they could not free themselves" (102). The revolution that made the peasants proprietors also made them resent the tax burden. It was not, therefore, the heaviness but the lightness of the feudal yoke that explains the violent explosion of 1789.

Equally indicative of the weakness of French feudalism prior to the revolution was that the nobility did not rule in the countryside. The parish, the rural equivalent of the township, was administered by either locally elected officials or, more frequently, those under control of the central power. The noble had lost all real power and authority in the community; yet he retained certain privileges that became a major source of resentment. The "people" detested the monarchy for the taxes it imposed and the nobility for its exemption from the taxes — a privilege now appearing totally unjustified because this class served no apparently useful function in the community. Unlike their English and German counterparts, the French nobles had ceased "to have anything to do with public administration save the administration of justice" (103). Even here, however, the state had taken over these functions to such a degree that the lords who still "exercised them regarded them less as a source of power and responsibility and more as a source of revenue." The French nobles had lost their power and made no apparently useful contribution to the community; for this reason, the privileges they retained appeared all the more odious.

The church also retained certain feudal privileges. Indeed, it was precisely its secular involvements in the old order that engendered the hatred of the people. It was not as a religious institution, but primarily as a political one that Christianity had provoked so violent a reaction. Yet, "throughout Europe precisely the same feudal rights were in force and, indeed, in most countries of the Continent weighed more heavily than in France" (105). Why, then, "did the very same feudal rights excite in the hearts of the French people a hatred so strong that it has survived its object and appears inextinguishable?" (105). So we come to the substance of Tocqueville's thesis: it was, paradoxically, the relative emancipation of the French cultivator that made him so resentful of the much diminished feudal prerogatives. For if the peasant had not become a landowner, and had remained under the lord's control, feudal rights would have seemed quite natural and, therefore, much less onerous.

Tocqueville's explanation, then, rests on an analysis of the changing relations of the two main classes of rural France and the consequent social psychology of the peasants, who had sunk their very beings into their little plots but who met on every side the interference of an arbitrary, arrogant, and parasitic lord. Various aspects of the feudal economic organization — tolls, dues, taxes, etc. — remained in force long after feudalism had ceased to be a political-administrative institution; this condition largely accounted for "the great hatred and envy that accumulated in the peasant's heart" (106). Feudalism was now hated more than in its heyday because "the very destruction of some of the institutions of the Middle Ages made those that remained a hundred times more odious" (106). This, then, is how Tocqueville explained the hostility of the people toward the nobility — the conflict between "democracy" and "aristocracy," in his original language.

ADMINISTRATIVE CENTRALIZATION

In his attempt to show (contrary to prevailing opinion and contrary even to the opinion he himself had only recently held) that the immense concentration of administrative power in France was not the creation of either the revolution or the Napoleonic era but rather of the old regime, Tocqueville links the phenomenon to class relations. The nobility had lost its power to the central authority — but this was a function of the democratic revolution. The point almost gets lost in his discussion because he is now more interested in the centralization of authority than in the accompanying phenomenon, to which he calls attention but whose implications he does not pursue. The center of power, the Royal Council, he writes, "was composed not of great seignorial lords but of persons of middle-class or even low extraction . . ." (109). This powerful but inconspicuous council, staffed by the bourgeoisie, controlled "everything that had to do with money, that is almost the entire administration of the country . . ." (109).

In the provinces as well, real authority passed from the nobles to the Intendants — men of "humble extraction" appointed by the central government. The Intendant was "all-powerful" and yet his power remained remarkably inconspicuous, because although he had his hand in everything he was hardly noticed beside the still lustrous old feudal aristocrats (110). The central authority controlled either directly or indirectly virtually every aspect of provincial and local life including public order and even public works of purely local interest. Thus what had earlier been, under the feudal system, the lord's obligations to the peasant, contributing to the rapport between the two classes, now came under the control of the central power. By increasing its intervention in the social life of the local community, the state not only usurped the lord's traditional functions, thereby undermining his rapport with the peasant, but also increased immeasurably the fiscal burden upon the people.

Even under the old order, however, the towns continued to govern themselves long after the lords had lost their political-administrative powers and responsibilities. The towns were like "small democratic republics whose officials were freely elected by the people and responsible only to them; municipal and public life was active and the inhabitants were proud of their rights and jealous of their independence" (115). With time, however, municipal autonomy also succumbed to the central power. In 1692 free elections were abolished by royal edict and "the king now sold to some of the inhabitants of each town the right to govern in perpetuity all the others" (115). What struck Tocqueville as altogether shameful about this development was that it was done not out of fear of the people, but for money.

Originally, for example, during the fifteenth century, the *corps de ville,* or executive, had been elected by all the townsfolk. By the eighteenth century, however, it was no longer the whole people but an assembly of representatives that elected the executive. The representatives, moreover, were neither elected by the people nor in sympathy with them. Tocqueville's comments on this process show that he found himself able to be more magnanimous toward the common people of the past than those who were his contemporaries. "These assemblies," he observes, "soon became almost exclusively bourgeois, admitting virtually no artisans. As a result the people, not so easily deceived as one might imagine, ceased to interest themselves in local government and became estranged from the affairs of the commune" (117). Thus what began as municipal democracy degenerated into oligarchy, which the Intendants recognized and called attention to — but which they sought to remedy by increasing central control even further (118).

Parallel to the early municipal autonomy, a form of village autonomy had also existed in the early Middle Ages. However, the villages suffered the same fate and eventually fell under the sway of the central power. Before the small village community succumbed, however, it was administered in a manner surprisingly similar to the rural townships of North America. Tocqueville now believed he may have erred in his *Democracy* when he had attributed a New World origin to the democratic features of its small communities. Free institutions, he now suggests, originated in the old world but they flourished so well in America because they were able to develop unhampered by either a seignorial system or a strong central government (119–120).

By the eighteenth century, village autonomy virtually disappeared and parish officials often became agents of the central power. The seignorial lord by now played no administrative role in the community and had no power. More, his privileged presence not only hindered good government but polarized the community because "the wealthy and cultivated residents increasingly fled to the towns leaving behind only the ignorant peasants incapable of directing the administration of local affairs" (120–121). The same process that led to the domination of the towns and rural parishes from the center also affected every other institution and corporate body. The reality, if not the term, "paternal government" had already existed under the old regime (122).

A highly centralized administrative authority was therefore an integral part of the pre-revolutionary French social structure. This authority soon came to supervise almost every detail of provincial and local government and effectively supplanted the authority of the nobility. The latter, then, already before the revolution had become a "former ruling class" that retained its rank, title, and certain seignorial privileges, but had lost its power. A major cause of the growth of the centralized state machine was that it had become an instrument of the democratic revolution long before the upheaval of 1789; it was a creation of the revolution, not the Revolution — the latter merely having retained, consolidated, and perfected the instrumentalities of the centralized state.

The immense state bureaucracy, which developed under the old regime largely as a function of the struggle for power, and which thus acted quite naturally in gathering unto itself as much power as possible, was far from efficient: "At least a year would elapse before a parish obtained authorization from Paris to repair a church steeple or the priest's house;

and more often than not it would take two or three years to honor local requests" (130–131). And when the government recognized this and, therefore, the "justice of the complaints," it nonetheless insisted that all the administrative formalities were necessary and indispensable. Tocqueville rejected this bureaucratic ideology, which he regarded as middle class as the administration itself. "The administrative functionaries," he wrote, "almost all bourgeois, already formed a class with its own particular spirit and traditions, code of honor and pride. Indeed, this was the aristocracy of the new and thriving social order which had already formed and waited only for the Revolution to assure it of its place" (132). The bureaucratic machine manned by the bourgeoisie by the eighteenth century had already succeeded in eliminating all intermediate forms of authority between the centralized state and the private individual. The centralized state bureaucracy was not created but rather reestablished after the revolution and wielded by the bourgeoisie for its own purposes.

By the mid-eighteenth century, centralization had gone so far that Montesquieu, whom Tocqueville quotes, had noted: "In France there is only Paris and a few outlying provinces Paris has not yet had time to devour" (139). Moreover, Paris, Tocqueville observed, had become the center of the French bourgeoisie and "a manufacturing city," a change that, together with the political hegemony of Paris, was destined to have formidable consequences (141). Of course, these consequences to which he refers were those that resulted from the concentration in Paris of industrial workers whose number had more than doubled in the sixty years prior to the revolution, "while in the same period the general population of the city grew by hardly a third" (142).

Tocqueville also observed that among the important reasons for the gravitation of industry to Paris was that "the fiscal authorities imposed fewer constraints on industry there than elsewhere; and nowhere was it easier to evade the control of the guilds than in the capital" (142). And when the government took alarm at the growing number of "manufactories, mills, and blast furnaces" in Paris it was for the wrong reason: it feared the increasing consumption of wood might lead to a fuel shortage in the city. "No one, however," Tocqueville remarks ironically, "perceived the real dangers inherent in so great a concentration of labor. Thus Paris had become the master of France while the army that was eventually to master Paris was already now assembling its forces" (142). But because this danger seemed, to Tocqueville, already to have passed, he had little more to say on the subject as he further explored the implications of administrative centralization and the predominance of Paris.

The old order had exhibited two contradictory aspects. On the one hand, there had seemed to be a growing social and cultural homogeneity among the upper and middle classes: nobleman and bourgeois came very much to resemble each other. Nobles were losing their traditional form of wealth to the Third Estate, selling their land, for example, "plot by plot, to the peasants, retaining only the seignorial dues which preserved the appearance rather than the reality of their former conditions" (145). The bourgeois was not only wealthier than the noble; his wealth often took the same form — land. Despite this, however, class differences and even cleavages became greater than before. Although noble and bourgeois appeared to be drawing closer they were in fact drawing apart, with the bourgeoisie growing increasingly hostile toward the nobility.

To explain this phenomenon, Tocqueville returns to an idea he first discussed more than twenty years earlier. The fundamental difference between the French and English social structure is best grasped if one understands that in France, as elsewhere on the continent, feudalism had led to the formation of an aristocracy of birth and of blood — a closed and rigid caste, whereas in England it evolved into a relatively open and flexible aristocracy. Not only did nobility and commoners join forces in business and politics; they intermarried — which is "even more significant." Tocqueville again illustrated the difference between the English and French social structures by showing how the words gentleman and *gentilhomme,* perhaps commonly derived, were now worlds apart — as far apart as their respective social worlds. The connotation of gentleman grew steadily wider in England as classes drew nearer and intermingled; in America, gentleman was applicable to all male citizens. The history of the term is thus "the history of democracy itself."

> In France [in contrast] the word *gentilhomme* has always remained confined to its primitive meaning. Since the Revolution it has dropped out of usage but has never altered its meaning. The word has been preserved intact to designate the members of a caste because the caste itself is as exclusive today as it has ever been (148–149).

Paradoxically, this caste-like tendency became even more pronounced in France after the bourgeoisie had penetrated the nobility and had taken over much of its wealth. The gulf between these classes grew steadily wider, despite the similarities between them. Earlier in French history, when feudalism had still been in full force, the third estate had had real power and responsibility in managing public affairs. If this had continued, perhaps France would have gone the English way. Instead, however, cooperation between noble and bourgeois broke down and "the two classes became not merely rivals, but enemies" (150).

This class hostility, Tocqueville suggests, was based not so much on conflicting material interests or on a struggle for power as on the privileges and prerogatives accorded the nobility. But his subsequent discussion shows that what he called privileges included material interest; the privilege resented most, he argues, was the nobility's "exemption from taxes which became more and more valuable from the fifteenth century up to the Revolution." The value of tax exemptions to the nobility was as great as the resulting financial burden imposed exclusively on the common people. The taxation policy exhibited particularly flagrant class discrimination. Unequal taxation stresses class differences as it creates a clear line of demarcation between those who benefit from the policy and those who suffer from it. Moreover, "each member of the privileged class perceives the real interest he has in not being confounded with the masses and in remaining firmly set apart from them" (152). In England, in contrast, there prevailed a relative absence of middle-class hostility toward the aristocracy, which could be explained not only by its openness but, more important, by its ill-defined boundaries. Everyone who hovered at its edge nursed the illusion that he would soon join the aristocracy or that he was already there.

In France, because of the inequalities, "ennobling commoners" increased class hostility, not because barriers between noble and commoner were insuperable but because the barriers were always visible and "once a man crossed them he was cut off from all outside the pale by privileges that were as onerous and humiliating to the commoners as they were profitable and honorific to him" (152). Thus, as the wealth and power of the nobility diminished, resentment and hostility toward it increased. To avoid the dreaded *taille,* the bourgeoisie more and more fled to the towns where, acting as a unified class, they could reduce the impact of the tax and occasionally even escape it altogether. This contributed to the conspicuously large number of towns in France but not to a great upsurge of business and industry; for place-hunting had become a widespread disease and the typical bourgeois therefore bought an official post instead of investing his money in business.

Estrangement and conflict of interest became equally evident between the bourgeoisie and the lower classes. The bourgeoisie managed to retain and develop political as well as economic privileges, because not only did they now enjoy certain exemptions from taxation, but they supported and initiated measures withdrawing political rights from the ordinary townspeople. It is worth noting, particularly in view of his own recent political past, that Tocqueville shows considerable scorn for those in power who opposed the voting and other rights of the humbler classes. Among the bourgeoisie, a degree of unity was already evident vis à vis the lower classes (155).

In this way, Tocqueville centers a substantial part of his analysis on the relationships among the various social classes. More, one of his central hypotheses is that along with "the destruction of political liberty, the separation of classes caused almost all the diseases from which the old regime perished" (159). In the first place the barriers were social. Tocqueville cites approvingly Arthur Young's opinion that the socializing one could have observed between an English duke and the plain farmers in the community, as infrequent, contrived, and superficial as this hobnobbing may have been, was quite unthinkable in France. The point was not that the English were less haughty, but rather that they recognized the necessity of making certain concessions to hold their power. For more important than token socialization were the very real economic sacrifices that the English aristocracy, as an enlightened and self-interested ruling class, had been prepared to make to ensure its rule: "The English aristocracy took upon itself the heaviest public charges in order that it should be allowed to govern; in France the nobility retained to the very end its exemption from taxes to console itself for having lost control of the government" (160).

However, as pointed out in the introduction to this chapter, Tocqueville did not place the responsibility for this development on the nobility alone. The policy originated with the kings not the nobility, the latter merely conniving in it. The kings chose the *taille* precisely because it was the most effective means of reducing the likelihood of conflict between the nobility and the monarchy. But the *taille* not only added substantially to the inequalities already existing, it "intensified the people's resentment of all the others." Thus the "monstrous consequence of sparing the rich and charging the poor" and an ever widening rift between the upper, privileged classes and the monarchy, on the one hand, and the oppressed poor, on the other. With "this division of classes, the crime of the late monarchy," the outcome was inevitable. For when "the various classes of the old order that had been isolated from one another for so long came once again into contact it was on their sore spots; they therefore sought to tear each other to pieces. Their mutual envy and hate survive to this day" (167).

The pre-revolutionary French social structure was therefore characterized by class alienation and hostility; and dominating the entire structure and in a sense causing the alienation and hostility was the great state bureaucracy. The latter, however, had not destroyed all freedom. A "spirit of resistance" (168) prevailed in the minds of many Frenchmen and among all classes. The nobility, the clergy, and the bourgeoisie could have asserted their independence and checked the state peacefully and nonviolently, had they so wished. The absolutism of pre-revolutionary France, Tocqueville reminds his reader, was not yet that of the Second Empire. The lower classes, however, "especially of the countryside, found themselves almost always unable to resist oppression otherwise than by violence" (175). As the condition of the lower classes, especially that of the French peasantry, was occasionally "worse in the eighteenth century than it had been in the thirteenth," and this "despite the progress of civilization" (178), there should be little wonder at the violent outburst of these classes.

The peasant, although something of a landowner and no longer subject to a feudal lord, was now worse off than before because he had been left behind by the other classes. The rich, whether noble or bourgeois, had abdicated their responsibilities to the peasant and abandoned the countryside while those who remained, having nothing of the old noblesse oblige but retaining innumerable privileges, treated him with the utmost disdain. The peasant, in turn, developed a deep-seated resentment toward all other classes, including even the priests: "By attaching themselves so firmly and visibly to the political hierarchy and sharing its privileges, they unavoidably came to share the hatred inspired by the temporal elites" (180). On all sides, the peasant was cold-shouldered and looked down upon, not to speak of the taxes, military service, and *corvée* — burdens he bore alone. In short, the "economic and social progress which was enriching all the other classes drove the peasants to despair; they and they alone were the victims of the advance of civilization" (185). The French peasants, then, "though they were free and, in a small way, landowners, remained almost as ignorant and often more miserable than the serfs, their forefathers" (187). Thus the largest class of French society developed less interest than any other in preserving the old order.

THE PHILOSOPHES

Why France had moved almost inexorably toward a great revolution could therefore best be understood by illuminating the class structure of the old order. However, another important and related aspect of the old social structure was the existence of a stratum of intellectuals who, Tocqueville believed, were different from both their English and German counterparts. Although the *Philosophes* had not actively and directly taken part in politics, as had the English, neither had they retreated into "pure philosophy and belles-lettres" as had the Germans. What was characteristic of the French men of letters was that although they were apparently removed from practical political problems and issues of government, they nonetheless probed the very foundations of society, examining its structure, and criticizing "its general plan" (193). In short, the *Philosophes* dealt in profoundly critical and revolutionary ideas. These ideas, moreover, far from being confined to intellectual circles, diffused throughout the society from the highest to the lowest classes, gripping, finally, the minds of the masses, and going so far as to fire the "imagination of women and peasants" (194).

Everyone now seemed to be pointing to the unreasonableness of existing institutions, while demanding that they be abolished and replaced by social forms and relations based on the rules of reason and natural laws. It was no accident that such revolutionary theories caught on in France at the time. With the prevailing abuses, the alienation of classes, the absence of any real participation by the people in politics, it is no wonder that the only alternatives before the Frenchman seemed to be "between supporting everything or destroying the whole social system" (196).

This frame of mind was also at least in part a consequence of the degeneration of the French nobility into a caste. Having lost their power, they lost also their authority to guide public opinion. The *Philosophes* therefore filled the vacuum with ease. They took over the directions of public opinion, and no one could challenge their role. Tocqueville found even more remarkable that the nobility had regarded "the doctrines most hostile to their particular privileges and even to their very existence as ingenious *jeux d'esprit*" (196).

Neither the nobility nor the Crown, those destined to be the chief victims of the coming democratic upheaval, had any presentiment of it. Even the unfortunate Louis XVI continued to view the nobility as the main enemy of the throne, and the bourgeoisie and the people as his staunchest supporters. The ruling elite and the upper classes, having lost touch with the people, had no realization whatsoever of their radical estrangement from the here and now, nor of their determination to seek "the ideal world that the *Philosophes* had constructed" (199).

In eighteenth-century France, not only the upper classes, as in Germany, but the people as well had become radically estranged from the church and from religion. Indeed, "nowhere had irreligion become the general, ardent, intolerant and oppressive passion that it became in France" (202). Nor was there any thought of replacing the old religion with a new. It was not in religion as such, Tocqueville emphasizes, that one must seek the reasons for the vehemence of the attack but rather in the social conditions. It was not the religious shortcomings of the church that made it so hateful an institution, but rather its secular involvements and practices.

Although the people in general perceived this aspect of the church — how it supported the secular authority, condoning its vices and "investing it with her sacred aura" — the literary intellectuals were in most direct conflict with the religious hierarchy, which was not only the very antithesis of reason, but interfered in their lives directly through censorship, for example. Thus the *litterateurs,* in fighting for the freedom of all, fought first "their own cause and began by shattering the fetters that constricted them most severely" (204). And, ironically, as the writers were subjected only to partial constraints and were never totally suppressed, this policy "augmented their influence instead of diminishing it" (205).

The connection between religion and class interest was clear to Tocqueville. He reminds his readers that after the revolution the upper classes had lost their taste for subversive literature and ideas. And in a formulation not too dissimilar to one Marx could have written, Tocqueville adds: ". . . little by little religion regained its influence on all those who had something to lose from popular disorder, and unbelief disappeared, or at least hid its head the more these men perceived the threat of revolution" (206). During the final phase of the old régime, however, the very class that had the most to lose from the new ideas cultivated and even propogated them among the lower classes.

With the decline of religion, the new secular ideals, which had captured the popular imagination, took its place. In effect, the great faith of the *Philosophes,* "fundamentally transforming the entire social system and regenerating the species" (208), soon became the new secular faith of the masses. For the first time in history both secular and religious authorities were attacked and destroyed at once, which could be attributed not only to the ideas of the enlightenment and to the conditions that rendered the masses amenable, but also to the emergence of a new phenomenon: professional revolutionaries. Their appearance, Tocqueville cautions his reader, should not be regarded as an isolated or ephemeral development. On the contrary, "they have formed a new race of men who have perpetuated themselves and have spread out in all civilized countries, everywhere retaining the same characteristics and passions. They were with us then and are still with us today" (208).

The "physiocrats" or "Economists" were another important source of revolutionary ideas. These men were the economic ideologues of the rising bourgeoisie who, Tocqueville asserts, neglected private rights and worried only about "public interest." In their attack upon the traditional obstructions standing before the advance of commerce and industry, they had not recognized that they were destroying the social conditions of liberty, autonomous local and secondary powers, and other checks on the central power. They had not seen that without such countervailing forces, solid political guarantees of liberty were nonexistent. This essential pluralism had been disappearing before the increasingly centralized state machine — a process accelerated by the fact that the interests of the bourgeoisie and monarchy had coincided in opposing the ancient powers.

From the vantage point of the bourgeoisie and the economists the ancient powers and institutions were just so many inpediments, while the central power was indestructible. Hence, "it was not a question of destroying this absolute power, but rather of turning it to their own account" (212). Thus they were inadvertently preparing the way for tyranny, as Tocqueville wrote:

> This particular form of tyranny sometimes called "democratic despotism," was unknown in the Middle Ages but already familiar to the Economists who stood for the abolition of all hierarchy, all class distinctions, all differences of rank. The nation was to be composed of individuals, almost alike and entirely equal. In this undifferentiated mass legitimate sovereignty was solely to reside — but a sovereignty carefully divested of all agencies that would enable the nation to direct and supervise its government. For above the nation was a single power, its mandatary, that could do anything and everything in the people's name without consulting it; while the people had no real means of controlling or checking this power, short of revolution. What was in theory the subordinate agent of the people became in practice its master (213).

Tocqueville regards this view as prototypical of "socialism," and he was probably right insofar as he was referring to some followers of Saint-Simon and others at the time who displayed little or no concern for checks and balances and the question of freedom. Nevertheless, Tocqueville still uses "socialism" as a catchword. There was, furthermore, a conspicuous disparity between his words and deeds when it came to free association as a countervailing force. Although he advocated the principle in theory, he opposed it in practice, as we saw earlier, when it was the working class that wished to avail itself of association to check the powers of the employers and the state. If freedom meant independent action and controlling one's fate, then clearly Tocqueville simply preferred that some should be more free than others.

It is well known that one of Tocqueville's main theses in the *Old Regime* was that "the reign of Louis XVI was the most prosperous period of the monarchy" and that "this very prosperity hastened the coming of the Revolution" (218). Tocqueville shows how by 1780 the administration, through the Intendants, was mainly concerned with increasing the wealth of the provinces by planning roads, canals, trade, and industry. He also argues that in that period, although the laws were just as harsh as earlier, they were applied with leniency as were the methods of collecting taxes. Concern for the poor, he believes, was also now greater than before as evidenced in the establishment of "charity workshops" and the allocation of huge sums for poor relief (220).

Tocqueville's main argument, without his having stated it in so many words, however, is that capitalist development was now enjoying unprecedented growth. The prosperity to which Tocqueville refers was mainly that generated by the expansion of commerce and industry. Bordeaux had now become, in Arthur Young's opinion, a busier commercial center than Liverpool. The reasons Tocqueville gives for this conspicuous expansion of capitalism are similar to those Marx suggests: The centralized authority together with the weakened nobility provided the bourgeoisie with greater freedom to engage in its most characteristic activities. Conditions were created in which "every man could get rich if he so wished and preserve his fortune once having acquired it" (222).

Paradoxical though it may appear, Tocqueville argues, it was precisely in this period that discontent seemed to grow; prosperity seemed to promote unrest. Those areas of France "which were to become the principal centers of revolution were precisely those in which progress was most evident" (222). When one looked over the various provinces of the country, one found that where liberty, wealth, and reforms were greatest, so was the revolutionary movement; conversely, where the old régime was most firmly entrenched, one saw the "fiercest and most prolonged resistance to the Revolution" (223).

If one were to state Tocqueville's argument in Marx's terms it would read something like the following: in those areas least exposed to "modernization," i.e., to the new mode of production and exchange of the bourgeoisie, the people knew only the old order, nothing else and certainly nothing better. Their consciousness was as stable as their way of life. In those areas, however, in which the modern mode of production had taken hold, the old order and methods were challenged at the root; social relations were in a state of flux; the contrasts between the old and new became clear for everyone to see; bourgeois practices generated bourgeois values — an insatiable appetite for material wealth.

The growing wealth of the bourgeoisie undermined its relation with its erstwhile ally, the monarchy. The latter's seemingly unlimited budgetary requirements were met by borrowing immense sums from the bourgeoisie; but now when the interest on the debt was not paid on time or not paid at all, this class grew more and more impatient and indignant. The indignation was not due to the delinquencies as such which were not new after all. Rather, it was due to the delinquencies in a new situation in which the government "had become the greatest consumer of the products of industry and the chief employer of labor in the kingdom." The taste for comfortable living that accompanied the expansion of commerce and industry now made the bourgeoisie's grievances intolerable.

> Thus it happened that *rentiers,* merchants, manufacturers, other men of business and financiers — ordinarily the class that opposes political change and befriends the prevailing government . . . now lost their patience and became the strongest advocates of reform. With a great hue and cry they called for a complete revolution in the financial system, not realizing that so profound a change of this aspect of the régime was bound to lead to the downfall of the régime as a whole (225).

Thus Tocqueville, in terms quite similar to those of Marx, viewed the eruption of 1789 as a bourgeois revolution, an issue to which we shall return in a later discussion.

It was the bourgeoisie and the monarchy that imparted to the masses a revolutionary consciousness. The privileged acted as if those in the lower classes were deaf and dumb. For it was precisely those who had most to fear from the masses who employed a highly colored rhetoric to describe the misery and poverty of the people, thus intensifying their resentment. Thirteen years before the revolution the king himself sounded like a revolutionary — even a revolutionary socialist — when he described the consequences of forced labor:

> By forcing the poor man alone to maintain the roads and to give his time and his labor without compensation, one is depriving him of the sole means he has of avoiding poverty and hunger and, therefore, compelling him to work for the profit of the rich (226).

Intendants denounced the rich "who owe to the labor of the poor all they possess. . . ." And the king again: "His majesty will defend the people

...st all maneuvers designed to deprive them of the barest necessities / forcing them to work for any wage that the employers see fit to give. The King will not tolerate a situation in which one part of the nation suffers as a consequence of the greed of the other" (227). Similarly, when he attempted to abolish the restrictions of the guild system, he declared: ". . . the right to work is a man's most sacred possession and any law that violates this natural right should be considered null and void. The existing trade and craft corporations are artificial and tyrannical institutions, the products of egoism, cupidity, and violence" (227). And Tocqueville observes that the masses soon came to see clearly the disparity between the rhetoric and the practice: "Such words were perilous indeed but all the more so as they were uttered in vain. For a few months later both the guilds and *corvée* were reinstated."

Thus trying to convince itself of the expediency of reform, the elite succeeded in teaching the masses that their superiors were responsible for the evils they were suffering, while the most objectionable features of the system remained intact and the elite continued to show its contempt for the lower orders. Tocqueville cites the conduct of Mme. Duchatelet who felt no embarrassment "while undressing in the presence of her manservants, being unable to convince herself that valets were real men" (228). In this way the dominant classes conducted themselves with a curious mixture of sympathy and contempt; they themselves exposed the abuses of their rule but continued to rule abusively; they talked of reforms but made none — or at least none with any positive effect. This was the great folly of the privileged and powerful who thought they were talking to themselves and that no one else was listening but who in actuality were creating their own gravediggers.

The revolution was therefore a foregone conclusion because of the great class antagonisms. Little tangible had been done by the privileged classes to diminish inequalities or abolish the worst abuses. The nobility retained its privileges to the very end and thus effectively isolated itself; the bourgeoisie became increasingly ambitious and impatient; and the monarchy brought centralization to such an extreme that he who captured Paris could dominate all France. When, finally, the old order was destroyed, even the most feeble checks on the central bureaucracy were destroyed with it. The new, post-revolutionary state power became more absolute than that of any French king, and ultimately, Tocqueville believed, this power was the fundamental condition that conduced to the despotism of his time.

One can little doubt the analytical brilliance of the *Old Regime* and the overall cogency of its thesis — or, more correctly, theses. One should, however, mention some findings of subsequent research that require a modification of Tocqueville's conception of events before the revolution. Economic historians, notably Henri Sée and C. E. Labrousse,[5] force us to qualify in several important respects Tocqueville's view that the reign of Louis XVI was a golden age of the old order, and that it was precisely the prosperity of his reign that hastened the revolution.

In his *Old Regime* as in his other works Tocqueville gave little attention to economic conditions; one could never learn from this study that a severe agricultural and industrial crisis had struck France in 1788–89. As a consequence of bad harvests, cereals in that year were more expensive than at any time since 1734. Prices rose incessantly until July 1789, and the high prices for grain, though disastrous for all "small people," were especially so for the peasants, many of whom could not grow enough to live on. At the same time an industrial crisis in the towns caused widespread unemployment "at the very moment when the cost of living was going up. Workmen could obtain no increase in wages." [6] The shortage of grain, the high cost of living, and chronic unemployment made mendicity "an incurable evil." Begging, which had been a permanent and respectable occupation under the old order, increased phenomenally with the crisis. Forced to leave their own parishes, beggars descended in large numbers upon the towns seeking relief. In 1790, "some 10,000,000 of the French people out of 23,000,000, were in need of relief, and . . . 3,000,000 of these were . . . considered paupers, i.e., beggars." Matters were perhaps worse in the countryside where "homeless persons banded together and resorted to threats and actual violence." [7]

The economic crisis aggravated to an extreme the monarchy's chronic financial troubles, because it reduced the government's revenue when it was most sorely needed, while increasing expenses, grain now "having to be purchased abroad by the state." [8] George Lefebvre attributes considerable

---

[5] See Henri Sée, *Evolution Commerciale et industrielle de la France sous l'ancien régime* (Paris, 1925); also his *Histoire économique de la France* (Paris, 1939); C. E. Labrousse, *La Crise de l'économie française à la fin de l'ancien régime et au début de la Revolution,* vol. I (Paris, 1944).

[6] George Lefebvre, *The Coming of the French Revolution,* translated by R. R. Palmer (Princeton, N.J.: Princeton University Press, 1967), pp. 104–105.

[7] *Ibid.*, p. 108.

[8] *Ibid.*, pp. 21–22.

importance to the economic crisis because it made the lives of the masses almost unbearable. Material want was a major motive in the 1789 riots, which, indeed, achieved their purpose, a reduction in the price of bread. The revolts of the people helped "dislocate the administration of the old regime" and strengthened the hands of the bourgeoisie. Undoubtedly, "economic distress should be included among the immediate causes of the Revolution." [9]

However, apart from the economic crises of 1788 – 89, Tocqueville's proposition that ". . . the social order that a revolution destroys is almost always better than the one immediately preceding it," [10] must be seriously questioned or, again, qualified. Most probably the eighteenth century was an era of great economic growth, especially for commerce and industry, although there is dispute about the last decade or so of the monarchy. Although C. E. Labrousse sees a widespread depression in both industry and agricultural beginning about 1778, Henri Sée describes unusual growth in big industry during the last two decades of the old order.[11] But even if we accept the latter view, that the two decades preceding the revolution were prosperous, an important question still remains: Who benefited from the commercial and, to a lesser extent, industrial expansion? *Who* was becoming more prosperous? Most probably not the people. "Between the two periods 1726–1741 and 1785–1789," writes George Lefebvre "it appears that prices had risen 65 percent and wages only 22 percent." While rural rents had risen even more than prices, "98 percent compared with 65 percent." [12] It was particularly the clergy, the nobility, and the rich more generally who benefited from this development as well as from the tax exemptions, as Tocqueville himself had noted, while the masses bore the severe burden of their diminishing purchasing power.[13]

And although Tocqueville was undoubtedly right in emphasizing that the French peasant of the eighteenth century was no longer a serf and had become something of a landowner, Tocqueville did overlook that a very large proportion of the French peasantry were tenant farmers, share-

---

[9] *Ibid.*, pp. 101–102.

[10] *L'Ancien Régime, op. cit.,* p. 223.

[11] Cf. Barrington Moore, Jr., *Social Origins of Dictatorship and Democracy* (Boston: Beacon Press, 1968), p. 68.

[12] Lefebvre, *op. cit.,* p. 23.

[13] Tocqueville's proposition may have some validity after all but in another sense which we shall consider later in a different context.

croppers, and propertyless agricultural laborers. The number of propertyless rural proletarians was not negligible. It "has been estimated," writes Lefebvre, "at about a fifth of family heads in Limousin, 30 to 40 percent in the Norman woodlands, 70 percent around Versailles and as high as 75 percent in maritime Flanders." [14] Even when they acquired a small patch of land, this changed their actual condition hardly at all. The "holdings of the overwhelming majority of the peasants," according to Lefebvre, "were not large enough to support them and their families." [15]

The inadequacy of the holdings may be explained partly by the backward cultivation methods that prevailed. Nonetheless, Lefebvre continues:

> In the region later comprised in the department of Nord nine families out of ten had too little to live on. The situation had grown worse since the middle of the eighteenth century, for the population had increased perceptibly, probably by three million. The number of proletarians had risen, while through division of inheritances the shares of property owners had become smaller. There was, therefore, at the end of the old regime, an agrarian crisis.[16]

In addition, during the second half of the eighteenth century, manorial lords increasingly encroached on the peasants' collective rights. In certain provinces the lords broke up and enclosed the commons; they "denied the right of vacant pasture on their own lands, while continuing to send their herds on to lands belonging to peasants." [17] Finally, there were the grievances that Tocqueville himself had underscored: almost alone the peasants shouldered the burdens of the *taille,* military service, road work, and military transportation. From the peasant "came most of the proceeds of the poll-tax and the twentieth-taxes." [18] Although the peasants were critical of the bourgeois for evading their proper share, they "were most especially aroused to a state of fury by the privileges of the aristocracy." [19] For notwithstanding that some peasants suffered more than others from the tithes and manorial dues, the peasants as a whole came to resent their feudal obligations even more than the royal taxes.

Alfred Cobban, whose work we shall consider more fully in a later context, also points to the "pressure of the unpropertied populace on those

---

[14] Lefebvre, *op. cit.*, p. 132.

[15] *Ibid.*, p. 133.

[16] *Ibid.*, p. 134.

[17] *Ibid.*, p. 141.

[18] *Ibid.*, p. 135.

[19] *Ibid.*, p. 136.

with property." [20] Along with the general population growth there was "a great increase in the numbers of the poor — the landless, craftless, statusless workers in both country and town." So great was the increase of the poor that "An examination of the *taille* lists for 1785 in 22 parishes in the neighborhood of Caen, taking the assessment of 5 livres as the poverty line, has shown that nearly half the total population did not reach this figure." In the region of Rouen, of a population of 16,548, some 2,530, or a minimum of 14 percent, were indigent. A sign of the times was the "flood of children abandoned by their parents." [21]

In short, commerce and industry may have expanded under Louis XVI, and the period of his reign may indeed have been a prosperous one. However, it also seems evident that for many it was a period of growing impoverishment and oppression.

Of course, Tocqueville acknowledged that the prosperity of the eighteenth century had its contradictions. He drew attention to the misery and oppression of the poor: the discriminatory tax policy, the burden of *corvée,* the basic inequalities in the administration of justice, the arrogance of the upper classes, and the intensified pressure of the lord on the peasant. Accompanying the prosperity, then, was a situation in which the peasant was in many significant respects worse off than his forefathers, the serfs. "They benefited not at all from the prodigious advance of the industrial arts and remained backward and uneducated in a social order of growing enlightenment." [22] They were as backward as the agricultural methods they employed, "those of the tenth century," according to an English expert whose opinion Tocqueville approvingly cites. The peasants of the eighteenth century had been left behind: ". . . the progress of society, that was enriching all other classes, drove them to despair. It was as if civilization had turned against them and them alone."[23] In these terms prosperity may indeed have hastened the revolution — by making the poor more aware of their own condition, thus causing their interest in preserving the old order to progressively diminish. This may be one meaning of Tocqueville's proposition but there is still another, to be considered later.

The eighteenth-century prosperity was enjoyed therefore by the upper classes, the bourgeoisie, but also certain sections of the nobility. The

[20] Alfred Cobban, *The Social Interpretation of the French Revolution* (Cambridge: Cambridge University Press, 1968), p. 133.

[21] *Ibid.,* pp. 133–134.

[22] *L'Ancien Régime,* pp. 187–188.

[23] *Ibid.,* p. 185.

embourgeoisement of the nobility and the "feudalization" of the middle class had now become quite pronounced. The nobility became increasingly dependent on money, while the typical bourgeois invested his money in land and public offices — judicial, financial, administrative, military, and municipal. Thus if before the eighteenth century the demarcation had been relatively clear between the old nobility (the so-called nobility of the sword) and the nobility of recent bourgeois origin, the differences between the two categories was now somewhat blurred.

The older nobility's need for money, "the lure of dowries," accelerated its assimilation with the new. Many nobles were won over by the bourgeois spirit and sought to profit from the advance of capitalism. Manorial lords largely controlled the right to grant mining concessions on their estates. "Timber and water rights for the most part belonged to the manorial domains, they were indispensable in the eighteenth century to iron-smelting and glass-making, as well as other types of manufacture. Some noblemen invested in industry." [24]

Tocqueville grasped the transformation in the eighteenth century of the nobility as a consequence of its dependence on money and the bourgeoisie; he noted, as well, the paradox that although bourgeois and nobleman were becoming more and more alike in many ways, the chasm between them increasingly widened, as did the breach between the middle class and the people. Tocqueville may have erred, however, in believing that in "no other period of French history was nobility so easily acquired as in 1789. . . ." [25] He overlooked what is often referred to as the "feudal reaction" of the eighteenth century. For it was only a minority of the nobles who, for the want of money, were either drawn to the bourgeoisie or declassed. Most lords, according to Lefebvre, "demanded their feudal rights with a new rigour" and tightened their grip on the peasants. He writes:

> They farmed out their rights to bourgeois agents who were relentless in collection of dues; they had minutely detailed manor-rolls drawn up, putting into effect dues which had become obsolete; they prevailed upon the king to issue edicts allowing them to appropriate a third of the common lands or to enclose their own fields and forbid the peasants to pasture their animals in them; they made use of the "planting right" to set out trees along the roads on land belonging to the peasants; they expelled the peasants from the forests.[26]

---

[24] Lefebvre, *op. cit.*, p. 13.
[25] *L'Ancien Régime,* p. 153.
[26] Lefebvre, *op. cit.*, p. 14.

At the same time the nobility regained control of the royal administration. Intendants were no longer the men "of humble extraction" Tocqueville believed they were, having assumed, erroneously, that things had not changed much in this respect since the regime of Louis XIV. With the exception of Necker, "all of Louis XVI's ministers were nobles. So were the members of his councils." The army, the navy, the church, the parlements the Intendancies, in a word all the command posts of the state, were now dominated by the nobility.[27]

A quite different criticism of Tocqueville's work relates to his description of the *philosophes* as abstract speculators, impractical men who were remote from actual political affairs and problems. The work of Daniel Mornet and of Peter Gay [28] have shown the errors in this conception, which Tocqueville probably took over uncritically from Burke. There were definite practical sides to the interests and work of both Rousseau and Voltaire, for example. Rousseau not only used Geneva as a model for his social contract; he gave quite practical political advice, when it was solicited, to the Polish monarchy.

Finally, Tocqueville attributed the great centralization in France solely to internal causes and ignored the contribution of foreign wars and foreign policy to the concentration of power by the state. However, all these criticisms, which are more in the nature of correctives, do not detract in any fundamental way from the quality of *L'Ancien Régime*. It remains a classic study of the old order and the social origins of the revolution.

[27] *Ibid.*, pp. 16–17.

[28] See Daniel Mornet, *La Pensée française au XVIIIe siècle* (Paris, 1926); see also his *Rousseau, l'homme et l'oeuvre* (Paris, 1950), and *Les Origines intellectuelles de la Révolution française* (Paris, 1933). Peter Gay's *Voltaire's Politics, the Poet as Realist* (Princeton, N.J.: Princeton, University Press, 1959), pp. 7–18, explicitly corrects Tocqueville's conception.

8. The Theory of Bourgeois Revolution

AN IMPORTANT ISSUE raised by the history of the French Revolution is the nature of its consequences and the validity of a theory to describe them. Georges Lefebvre, whose study I have relied on for the critical corrections of Tocqueville's work, is undoubtedly among the greatest historians of the revolution. He recognized the enormous complexity of both the French social structure under the old order and the revolutionary process that destroyed it. As the revolution unfolded it revealed its manifold aspects: the occasionally compatible and occasionally conflicting interests of the participating classes and strata, as well as the diverse consequences for each. The revolution developed in successive stages that one may label for convenience the aristocratic, bourgeois, popular, and peasant revolutions. Yet all these ultimately furthered the economic and political interests mainly of one class — the bourgeoisie. Lefebvre writes: "The Third Estate was a purely legal entity in which the only real elements were the social ones — and of these the most important, the one which led and mainly benefited from the Revolution, was the bourgeoisie." [1] And in *Etudes sur la Révolution Française,* he writes: "The revolution is only the crown of a long economic and social evolution which has made the bourgeoisie the mistress of the world." This justifies, in Lefebvre's view, the term "bourgeois revolution."

This concept is precisely that which another eminent historian of the French Revolution, Alfred Cobban, regards as a kind of ideological straitjacket into which the historical facts have been forced. Cobban objects to

---

[1] Georges Lefebvre, *The Coming of the French Revolution* (Princeton, N.J.: Princeton University Press, 1967), p. 41.

the concept and to the accompanying theory — actually a philosophy of history, he believes — according to which the revolution is explained as the victory of the middle class over the feudal nobility, climaxing a long development in which the steadily rising bourgeoisie finally destroyed feudalism. This, by now, is the "perfect cliché" that "every schoolboy knows" [2] — a cliché, moreover, which has become the orthodox interpretation or established theory shared, interestingly enough, by ideologically diverse schools of historiography. This theory of the revolution was first put forward by the revolutionaries themselves, later elaborated by such restoration historians as Guizot, and, finally, "taken for granted in most of the work that has since been done on the history of the revolution. . . ." [3]

So although Cobban concentrates his fire on the Marxists and mainly on Lefebvre (whom he nonetheless respects as "one of the greatest of French historians of this century") for having allowed himself to be seduced by Marxian sociological dogma, and for abandoning the strict empirical posture of his youth, the questions Cobban raises and the criticisms he makes apply as well to other historians who have adopted the established theory or major aspects of it. His critique could apply to Tocqueville's work, though Cobban never mentions Tocqueville by name. Tocqueville's work does, however, deserve attention in light of Cobban's thesis that "the interpretation of the revolution in terms of the overthrow of feudalism by the bourgeoisie, always rather meaningless, — [is] becoming increasingly incompatible with the results of modern research."

After all, Tocqueville also held the theory (or philosophy of history) that democracy was inexorably destroying aristocracy; in the *Old Regime* he used less vague concepts and interpreted the revolution in terms quite similar to those Cobban describes as established. Indeed, this is so much the case that Lefebvre, the "Marxist," regards Tocqueville as a kindred spirit and important forerunner who explained France's fateful history by the evolving relationships of her social classes. Let us therefore first summarize Cobban's thesis and then have another brief look at the *Old Regime* in its light.

THE MEANING OF FEUDALISM

Cobban acknowledges that historians have not simply fabricated the idea that the revolutionaries of the eighteenth century had believed feudalism

---

[2] Alfred Cobban, *The Social Interpretation of the French Revolution* (Cambridge: Cambridge University Press, 1968), p. 25.

[3] *Ibid.*, p. 8.

was the enemy. They no doubt held deeply felt grievances against something they called feudalism. "The problem," however, "is to identify their grievances and discover what, if anything, was feudal about them."[4] This is a reasonable question and no mere terminological quibble, Cobban believes, because the Constituent Assembly, when it had decided to abolish feudal rights, had great difficulty in deciding what was feudal and in distinguishing it from the nonfeudal.

Here we cannot, of course, review all the details of Cobban's argument. It will suffice, for our purposes, to summarize it. During the Middle Ages, although land passed rapidly from the nobles to the *roturiers* (men of bourgeois origin), the latter had no feudal rights over the land. A careful distinction was made between the *domaine direct* of the seigneur and the *domaine utile* of the commoner. By the eighteenth century, however, although the seigneur still retained the rights of *seigneurie,* ownership of the landed property was now firmly in the hands of the so-called tenant who was now the real proprietor. Furthermore, seignorial rights themselves soon passed into non-noble hands so that *"roturiers* came to exercise rights of *seigneurie."* [5] Thus the ownership of both land and seignorial rights, in an earlier age the exclusive prerogatives of the nobility, were now "separable from noblesse as a personal quality."

In addition, some nobles had slid from their traditional position in still other respects: "In Brittany nobles are found as steward, gamekeeper, wig-maker, chairman, muleteer. In Normandy nobles were in the *dépôts de mendicité."* On the other hand, there were great nobles with enormous wealth in land, investments, pensions, or official posts. Finally, some middle-class nobles had so thoroughly adapted themselves to bourgeois ways that they were hardly distinguishable from the bourgeois. The main points of Cobban's argument, then, are that by the eighteenth century the nobility had lost certain essential prerogatives; that it was a complex social category ranging from the very rich at one end of the continuum to the impoverished at the other; and that many nobles had become so intimately involved in commercial or capitalistic enterprises that they were indistinguishable from the middle class.

All these facts appear of course in Lefebvre's work and in the works of other Marxist historians, as Cobban is well aware. And Tocqueville undoubtedly understood all this. What then is Cobban's point? It appears to be "that the attack on feudalism cannot be equated with a simple

---

[4] *Ibid.*, p. 26.
[5] *Ibid.*, p. 28.

attack on the nobles as such." [6] If it was not an attack on the nobles, what was it? Was it perhaps an attack on the seignorial rights? This is the basic question for Cobban. For "if 'feudalism' in 1789 did not mean seignorial rights, it meant nothing."

THE ABOLITION OF SEIGNORIAL RIGHTS

That seignorial rights existed in the eighteenth century until they were abolished during the revolution Cobban accepts as well established historical knowledge. The problem, however, is, first, whether these rights may justifiably be equated with feudalism and, second, who abolished them. What he is mainly challenging here is that part of the established theory alleging that the bourgeoisie destroyed the system of seignorial rights. Again, Cobban is aware that Lefebvre knew the relevant facts. Indeed, he cites Lefebvre's observation that "up to 14 July 1789, the bourgeois had neither the desire nor the intention to attack the seignorial rights, and they had no idea of calling on the peasants to revolt, or of abolishing seignorial rights without compensation." [7] Yet the National Assembly, composed of nobles, clergy, and bourgeois, took the decisive step. How is this to be explained?

"It is accepted by practically all recent historians of the revolution," writes Cobban, "that what forced the National Assembly into the decisions of the night of the fourth of August was the widespread and alarming peasant revolt of the spring and early summer of 1789." This was no idealistic act on the part of the Assembly; far from it.

> A number of the more liberal but also more realistic, members of the Assembly had come to the conclusion, almost certainly a correct one, that unless concessions were made to the peasantry the whole of rural France would remain in a state of endemic rebellion. The generous gestures of 4 August were contrived in advance, and planned for a night session in the hope that many who might have resisted them would be absent.

But by August 11, members of the Assembly were having second thoughts, so that while they were emphasizing their intention of abolishing feudalism, *their real purpose was not to extend but to limit* "the scope of the changes," [8] as Cobban wishes to emphasize. Actually, it was the peasants who demanded the changes while the bourgeoisie resisted them.

What therefore needs to be explained is not why the bourgeoisie

---

[6] *Ibid.*, p. 33.

[7] *Ibid.*, p. 37.

[8] *Ibid.*, p. 39.

abolished the last remnants of feudalism, i.e., the system of seignorial rights, but rather why they opposed its abolition and then acquiesced under pressure. Bourgeois resistance and opposition to the changes is after all quite understandable if one recalls the facts: a great proportion of bourgeois wealth was in land and *seigneuries.* Even the so-called "feudal reaction" and particularly the intensification of pressure on the peasants was facilitated by bourgeois agents and tax-farmers. Because of these facts one might justifiably describe the "feudal reaction as less a reversion to the past than the application to old relationships of new business techniques." [9] The material interests of the bourgeoisie had therefore become so tied to the modified, commercialized, seignorial system that they might never have attacked it without the pressures of the peasants.

A similar observation may be made regarding the so-called *banalités,* the lords' control of the mill and oven and olive or wine press, a control which the peasants hated most among the seignorial rights. Apart from whether these rights may be regarded as feudal — Cobban prefers to view them "in more modern terms, as a commercial racket" — the *cahiers* of the towns showed no great interest in getting rid of the *banalités.* Then, some ground exists for interpreting the revolution in the countryside not as antifeudal but antibourgeois "directed partly against the penetration of urban financial interests into the countryside." [10]

WHO WERE THE REVOLUTIONARY BOURGEOIS?

Lefebvre has analyzed the eighteenth-century French bourgeoisie into five strata:

(1) the bourgeois proper "living nobly on his property"; (2) members of the royal administration; *officiers,* proprietors of venal offices, some of them ennobled; (3) lawyers — notaries, *procureurs, avocats;* (4) members of the liberal professions — doctors, scientists, writers, artists; (5) the world of finance and commerce — shipbuilders, wholesale traders, entrepreneurs, and the upper grades of financiers starting with the Farmers General.

First, Cobban objects to the vague and broad omnibus term "bourgeois," because it tends to obscure the differences among the strata as well as the differences in wealth and status within each stratum. In addition, "bourgeois," as employed in the established theory, conceals the fact

---

[9] *Ibid.,* p. 47.
[10] *Ibid.,* p. 52.

that the attitude toward the revolution varied both within and among the strata.

More important, however, is Cobban's thesis regarding the respective roles of these strata in the revolution. The bourgeoisie proper was conservative, not revolutionary. It was by wealth and way of life not unlike the "moderately prosperous noblesse and very largely shared its fate — whatever that was — in the Revolution." [11]

The commercial and financial interests were definitely increasing their wealth as they benefited most directly from the growing "prosperity of the eighteenth century." The largest of these, Cobban believes, probably were also conservative. What about the *"officiers,* holders of venal posts, lesser officials of the royal administration, lawyers and members of the liberal professions"? Of these, the only category about which there is sufficient knowledge to make a positive statement is the *officiers.* They were "definitely not rising in wealth" and maintaining their social status only with difficulty. So if one may speak of the financial and commercial classes as "rising" (Cobban dislikes the figure), then "the class of venal officers was declining. The inevitable result was a conflict between the rising and declining groups, which particularly took the form of a struggle for control of the towns." [12]

Although historians disagree on which stratum in the main led the revolution, Cobban believes, with Lefebvre, that it was "the *officiers* and the men of the liberal professions [who] prepared and directed the revolution. . . . This was the revolutionary bourgeoisie." [13] Lefebvre maintains, however, that although not directly led by the commercial, financial, and industrial bourgeoisie, it was their interests in the main that the revolution nevertheless served to advance.

ECONOMIC CONSEQUENCES OF THE REVOLUTION

One consequence of the revolution was the abolition of the privileged corporations in industry. It is not at all clear, however, argues Cobban, who gained and who lost by their abolition. Nor is it clear, as it so often assumed, that it liberated the economy from feudal fetters, thus contributing to capitalist development. Another consequence was the freeing of trade, but mainly in the sense of doing away with internal customs. Here, however, Cobban considers it important that the movement to

---

[11] *Ibid.,* p. 58.

[12] *Ibid.,* p. 59

[13] *Ibid.,* p. 61.

abolish these customs "was led throughout, and ultimately brought to success, not by the representatives of the commercial and industrial interests, but by reforming officials. . . .

". . . Manufacturing interests tended on the whole to support, and commercial interests to oppose, the reform."[14] More important, the revolution, far from accelerating industrial development, retarded it, and was, in addition, a disaster for France's colonial and foreign trade. Business and industry were, in 1815, not appreciably different from what they were in 1789 and no real industrial revolution occurred in France until the Second Empire. Correspondingly, it was not the commercial, financial, and industrial strata of the bourgeoisie that ruled France in the post-revolutionary era but rather a bourgeoisie of landowners — which helps us to understand why France was "such an intensely conservative society . . . for the next century and a half."[15]

In the remaining chapters, Cobban argues cogently that the revolution basically was an explosive manifestation of the resentment of the country against the town. The peasants had known that the seignorial dues "were often owned, and even more often collected, by the bourgeois." Peasant proprietors and tenants rose up against those who were oppressing them and in these terms it was a revolt "against and not for the bourgeoisie."[16]

The revolution and its aftermath, Cobban concludes, constituted a political revolution that overthrew the monarchy and created the Napoleonic state. Socially, however, it was a revolution not for but *against* the capitalist forces that now had begun to dominate the countryside — the antifeudal element having been quite negligible. The revolution was a revolt of the country against the town but also a consolidation of the general rights of property against the propertyless, of the power of the rich over the poor. It was the triumph in France of the "conservative, propertied, land-owning classes, large and small." And although the revolution effected certain humanitarian and democratic reforms and removed many old barriers that stood in the way of a unified and efficient modern state, "it also frustrated the movement for a better treatment of the poorest sections of the society, both rural and urban, which was manifesting itself in the last years of the *ancien régime*."[17]

---

[14] *Ibid.*, pp. 70–71.

[15] *Ibid.*, p. 90.

[16] *Ibid.*, p. 102.

[17] *Ibid.*, p. 170.

How, then, does Tocqueville's *Old Regime* appear in the light of Cobban's thesis? Of course, Tocqueville never lived to complete the study he had hoped to make of the "French Revolution itself" and "the new social order which issued from it."[18] Because he did, however, consider his finished work a study of the fundamental causes of the revolution, one may make several inferences regarding the theory of the "bourgeois revolution," and the degree to which he subscribed to it. To anticipate what we shall find, the point is not to argue that Tocqueville was right and Cobban wrong but merely to show that Tocqueville did utilize some major concepts and assumptions of the so-called established theory. Afterwards, we shall also address ourselves to the relative validity of the theory.

First among the questions Cobban raises is the meaning of feudalism, and whether historians who have subscribed to the orthodox interpretation have been justified in describing the institutions and relationships destroyed by the revolution as feudal. Of course, no serious historian of either Tocqueville's time or our own has regarded feudalism in the eighteenth century as if it had not changed since its heyday. Tocqueville states quite clearly that, by the eighteenth century, the ancient order of Europe had declined and disintegrated so far that it was "half in ruins." When he uses the term "feudal," therefore, he means what has remained of the old order in however modified a form — its vestiges. In Chapter 5 of Part I, entitled "What were the results of the French Revolution?" he wrote:

> . . . the effects of the Revolution were none other than to abolish those political institutions which for many centuries enjoyed an undivided hegemony throughout most of Europe. The Revolution abolished those institutions, commonly designated as feudal, in order to replace them with a social and political order at once more uniform and simple and based on the principle of equality.

And he continues:

> these old feudal institutions had still entered into and shaped the religious and political institutions of Europe and had, in addition, given rise to a host of ideas, sentiments, manners and morals that adhered to them. Thus a frightfully violent convulsion was required in order to excise these institutions from the social organism and to destroy them utterly.[19]

---

[18] Alexis de Tocqueville, *Oeuvres Complètes,* tome II, pt. 1, *L'Ancien Régime et la Révolution* (Paris: Gallimard, 1952), p. 250.

[19] *Ibid.,* p. 95.

And in the same vein:

> The Revolution entirely destroyed and is in the process of destroying
> (for the Revolution is still with us) everything in the old order that
> stemmed from aristocratic and feudal institutions, everything in any way
> connected with them or bearing their slightest imprint.[20]

So Tocqueville was not averse to using the term "feudal" to describe what
had remained of that order in the eighteenth century, and in his time as
well.

And, as we have already seen in our exposition of the main theses
of *L'Ancien Régime,* Tocqueville observed many of the phenomena to
which Cobban calls attention: the similarities between noblemen and
bourgeois (but also their differences); the fact that the bourgeoisie as
well as the nobility gained at the expense of the peasantry; the town vs.
the country; and, finally, the great gulf between rich and poor, generally.
And although Tocqueville centers attention throughout on the countryside and more specifically on the condition of the peasantry and their
alienation from the nobility, he also regards the growing discontent, particularly of the bourgeoisie and its agitation for reforms, as crucial for an
understanding of the revolution. It was this class, and particularly the
rentiers, financiers, merchants, and manufacturers, who were most directly
antagonized during the recurrent financial crises. As a result of the monarchy's chronic delinquency in paying its debts, these social elements
now became the most ardent advocates of reform. They called for a
revolutionary change of the financial system, thereby initiating a process
that soon led to the collapse of the ancient social structure in its entirety.
The bourgeoisie led the people in their onslaught upon the aristocracy
and the old regime, the destruction of which was the first great blow
struck by democracy in its inexorable and permanent advance. In these
terms, the events of 1789 constituted a bourgeois-democratic revolution.

THE FRUITFULNESS AND VALIDITY OF THE THEORY

How valid then is the theory of the bourgeois-democratic revolution, a
theory shared in many of its salient aspects by historians of diverse ideological convictions, including, as we have seen, certain Marxists as well
as Tocqueville?

Among the recent studies of the French revolution, that of Barrington Moore [21] appears most relevant to this question. Moore takes

---

[20] *Ibid.,* p. 96.

[21] Barrington Moore, Jr., *Social Origins of Dictatorship and Democracy* (Boston:
Beacon Press, 1967).

Cobban's objections into account (though without ever mentioning Cobban in this connection) and yet salvages the substance of the theory.

Why have some societies modernized in the context of liberal-democratic institutions while others have done so by revolutions from above that result in authoritarian régimes and fascism? This is one of the central questions of Moore's study. England, France, and the United States are the cases he considers as stages along the democratic route; Germany and Japan are examples of modernization by revolutions from above. Here, attention is confined to the French case.[22]

Moore begins by noting, as did Tocqueville, certain important differences between English and French social conditions. The English landed gentry and nobility had early gained independence from the Crown as well as sufficient power to check the central monarchy. The nobles, fusing with the expanding commercial and manufacturing classes, who had their own rather strong economic base, developed in the countryside a form of commercial agriculture that led to the disappearance of the peasantry and the peasant problem.

The French nobility, in contrast, had been drastically weakened by the central power long before the Revolution. Although there was some fusion with the bourgeoisie, the latter represented relatively undeveloped commercial and industrial interests. In response to the rising urban demand for grain and other food the noble extracted from the peasants all he could in kind and in cash. Neither the production of grain nor wine had wrought in France what wool-production had in England: a capitalistic type of agriculture, with its accompanying structural changes in the countryside. Indeed, production for the market in France reinforced the traditional patterns by which the noble controlled the peasant. Whereas the large English gentry had enclosed the land keeping their estates intact and leasing them to relatively big farmers who, in turn, employed landless agricultural laborers, "the French aristocrat kept the peasant on the land and used feudal levers to exact more produce. Then the nobleman sold the produce on the market." [23] Thus commercial agriculture in France led to results quite opposite from those in England. In France, production for the market, far from undermining feudal institutions,

---

22 However, the reader is urged to consult the whole of Moore's study since one cannot fully appreciate his analysis of the French case without the comparisons and contrasts he makes with all the others.

23 Moore, *op. cit.*, p. 48.

"infused a new life into old arrangements, though in a way that ultimately had disastrous consequences for the nobility." [24]

This was the situation toward the end of the old régime: peasants, on the one hand, working the land, and nobles, on the other, taking a share of the yield either directly in kind or indirectly in cash. At the same time, the noble contributed virtually nothing to the community, as Tocqueville had noted, because the central bureaucracy had increasingly usurped his social and political functions. Thus the French noble was neither a feudal lord in the older sense nor "yet a full-blown capitalist farmer. Essentially what the landed proprietor possessed were certain property rights, whose essence were claims, enforceable through the repressive apparatus of the state, to a specific share of the economic surplus." [25] So although the position of the French nobility had changed in response to capitalistic influences from the towns as well as to the monarchy's sustained efforts to curb and diminish its power, the nobles nevertheless retained considerable control over the peasants — despite the de facto property rights that they had acquired by the end of the eighteenth century.

An important aspect of the so-called "feudal reaction" was actually the extension into agriculture of commercial and capitalistic practices by feudal methods. Feudal rights and dues were restored where they had fallen into disuse mainly to obtain a larger share of the peasants' crops. The spread of capitalism into the countryside resulted in the greater exploitation of the peasantry, which was accomplished by the nobility with the support of royal absolutism. Similarly, the enclosures (with which the monarchy had experimented under pressure from the physiocrats), though not as prevalent as in England, benefited mainly the big landed interests, both noble and bourgeois.

Capitalism was therefore penetrating from all sides in eighteenth century France through the seignorial reaction as well as through the attack on feudalism. And capitalism in this form immeasurably increased peasant hostility and resentment toward the old régime because capitalism enhanced the unity of the old and new nobility, not as in England, outside and against the monarchy, but against the peasants. The more recently ennobled commoners, who employed feudal prerogatives and methods to increase the exploitation of the peasants, became staunch defenders of privilege and opponents of reform, and therefore also the

---

[24] *Ibid.*, p. 55.
[25] *Ibid.*

enemies of those "sections of the bourgeoisie that were not identified with the old order" — that is, those sections of the bourgeoisie who were demanding the removal of the feudal restrictions on trade.

The demands of these middle-class groups, expressed in the philosophy of the physiocrats and executed by the monarchy, turned all sections of the third estate against the monarchy and the nobility. Turgot's reforms of September 13, 1774, only parts of which had gone into effect, included a tax reform, free trade in grain, suppression of the *corvée* and the guilds, and the right of workers to choose their own occupations. Free trade in grain had raised the price of food, thereby antagonizing mainly the small consumers who rioted and demanded the reduction of bread prices. The essence of the popular demands was not to increase production but to restore the traditional controls in which "a benevolent authority would ensure a 'fair' distribution of necessities to the poor. This sentiment, based on the lower strata of the peasants and the urban plebs, the famous *sans-culottes,* was to be the main source of radical measures in the Revolution itself." [26] However, Turgot's policies also turned the upper strata of the urban bourgeoisie against the monarchy. The reforms were resented by the financiers because they had benefited more from the "corrupt feature of the bureaucracy" and resented by the manufacturers because Turgot had "refused to protect French industry. . . ." [27]

All major elements of the third estate, peasants, *sans-culottes,* and bourgeoisie, thus had severe grievances, and each element, for its own reasons, increasingly opposed the monarchy. Ultimately the combined pressure of all these social elements brought about the destruction of the old order. It cracked from the top down and the monarchy could no longer control the divisive forces.

The small, poor peasants were land-hungry. They wanted a plot if they had none and a larger plot if they already had some land. In addition they wished to preserve those customs of the village community which had traditionally made life more bearable for them. The peasants were hardest hit by the developments of the late eighteenth century and eventually became quite radical, joining hands with the radical movement of the towns. Prosperous peasants had enclosed the commons, steadily encroaching on the gleaning and pasture rights of the poor and even wiping out those rights altogether. The prosperous peasants also prevented the poor from dividing the land. In these terms, there "were at

---

[26] *Ibid.*, p. 69.
[27] *Ibid.*

least two peasant revolutions, that of the peasant aristocracy and that of the larger and more diffuse majority, each following its own course and also from time to time fusing [with] or opposing revolutionary waves in the cities." [28] The "peasant aristocracy" was discontented owing to its intermediate position between the nobility and the rural poor. What these upper strata of the peasantry wanted, judging from the *cahiers,* was to eliminate the "arbitrary aspects of the feudal system that had been increasing in the last years of the old order." [29]

The so-called feudal reaction together with the nobility's attempt to take over the state through the Estates-General tended, at least temporarily, to unify the diverse social elements of the third estate. Add to this the economic crisis just before the revolution, and what appears relatively clear is that with the *Grande Peur* (a great and widespread fear among the peasants of "brigands" as an instrument of an aristocratic conspiracy) "opposition to feudalism came to the surface everywhere. Even where the peasants did not rise, they refused their feudal obligations." [30]

The revolution itself developed in phases, beginning with the first offensive of the nobility and becoming more and more radical as it proceeded. The Parisian *sans-culottes* were the main impulse of each phase and each succeeded so long as it had peasant support. The propertied peasants, on the other hand, also set the limits of each radical surge because as soon as their interests appeared to be placed in jeopardy by the demands of the *sans-culottes,* and the poor more generally, the well-to-do peasants withdrew their support, "the radical revolution petered out, and its urban remnants were easily repressed."

"It is fair to hold," Moore continues, "that the peasantry was the arbiter of the Revolution, though not its chief propelling force. And even if it was not the main propelling force, it was a very important one, largely responsible for what in retrospect seems the most important and lasting achievement of the Revolution, the dismantling of feudalism." [31]

Thus Moore underscores that the main objective consequence of the Revolution was the destruction of the feudal system — or what was left of it. This was accomplished in several blows. The first came on August 4, 1789, when the Constituent Assembly — composed of men of property and law and order and quite recently saved by a popular uprising — under tremendous popular pressure passed the decrees that did away with many

---

[28] *Ibid.,* p. 73.

[29] *Ibid.*

[30] *Ibid.,* p. 75.

[31] *Ibid.,* p. 77.

feudal obligations. Although some feudal dues survived this blow, the Assembly nevertheless

> voted equality before the law, the abolition of feudal obligations that rested on persons (without indemnification), equality of punishments, the admission of all to public services, the abolition of the sale of offices, and suppression of the tithe (without indemnity). These were enough to justify the results of this famous occasion as [in Lefebvre's words] the 'death certificate of the Ancien Régime.'[32]

The second blow came after the uprisings of 1791–92 and as a consequence of them. Feudal dues were abolished without indemnity unless "the original title survived" and common lands, usurped by lords, were returned to villages. Still another decree sought to enable the rural proletarians to purchase small units of confiscated *émigré* properties. This, in particular, soon provoked the hostility of the richer peasants who attacked the decree as a form of communism of property. The split between rich and poor was sharpening.[33]

During the first two phases of the revolution the interests of the peasants and *sans-culottes* coincided in certain important respects and had the effect of prodding the bourgeoisie farther than it might otherwise have gone. However, this coincidence of interest, which enabled the radical and bourgeois revolutions to reinforce each other, could not last because a basic conflict of interests transcended all other temporary ones — that between the propertied and the propertyless. The split came in the third and final phase of the revolution, which then ground to a halt.

With the war, the shortage of food, soaring food prices, and the resulting starvation and discontent in the cities, the most urgent tasks confronting the revolutionary leaders were to get grain to the armies, to Paris and other big cities, and from areas of surplus to areas of short supply. The revolutionary government resorted to requisitioning and price controls and for a time these achieved the desired results. Eventually, however, these measures of the Committee of Public Safety (1793–94) turned the peasants, particularly the wealthier ones who produced substantial surpluses above their own needs, against the revolution. Requisitioning and price controls appeared, to these substantial peasants, as a direct and outright attack upon them. Why they should have thus regarded these measures, and turned against the government, becomes even

---

[32] *Ibid.*, p. 78.
[33] *Ibid.*, p. 80.

clearer when one recalls that the main agents of the government were revolutionary "armies" of townsmen and "outsiders."

If therefore the *sans-culottes* were able to push the Jacobin leaders into policies that saved the revolution, they could do so only by alienating the peasants; and without peasant support the revolutionary fervor of the *sans-culottes* was ineffectual, especially since the revolutionary government now had little or no reason to make concessions to the urban masses: the king and nobility were disposed of, or so it appeared, and the revolutionary armies had scored impressive victories at the frontiers.

> Hence the forces of order and property could and did use the army (which here moved against popular insurrection for the first time) to put down the last powerful surge of the *sans-culottes*. The repression that followed inaugurated the White Terror. No matter how radical the city was, it could no nothing without the help of the peasants. The radical revolution was over.[34]

Now, to return to the main question, what were the main accomplishments of the revolution and in what sense and in what degree may these accomplishments be described as a "bourgeois revolution"? As we have seen, Moore notes and acknowledges many facts that Cobban regards as fundamentally damaging to the theory of the "bourgeois revolution." He observes, for instance, the capitalistic aspects of the feudal reaction; the anticapitalist character of both agrarian and urban radicalism; the crucial role of the peasantry in the abolition of feudal dues and the reluctance of the bourgeoisie that acquiesced only under pressure; and, finally, the cleavages between town and country and rich and poor. At the same time, Moore agrees with the so-called established theory and with Tocqueville's judgment that the revolution virtually destroyed

> the whole interlocking complex of aristocratic privilege: Monarchy, landed aristocracy, and seignorial rights, a complex that constituted the essence of the *ancien régime*. It did so in the name of private property and equality before the law. To deny that the predominant thrust and chief consequences of the Revolution were bourgeois and capitalist is to engage in a trivial quibble.[35]

Moore goes on to emphasize, however, that what remains

---

[34] *Ibid.*, p. 92.
[35] *Ibid.*, p. 105.

questionable in the view that it was a bourgeois revolution is any argument to the effect that a relatively solid group of commercial and industrial interests had achieved enough economic power in the last quarter of the eighteenth century to throw off feudal shackles mainly by its own efforts in order to initiate a period of industrial expansion.[36]

In the course of its development, the revolution expressed the variety and complexity of the participating social forces. In the end, however, it "was a victory for an economic system of private property and a political system based upon equality before the law, the essential features in Western parliamentary democracies. . . ." [37]

Yet, if Moore agrees with Tocqueville that by destroying the aristocracy "the Revolution finished the work of the Bourbons," he disagrees, apparently, on the long-term significance of this fact for subsequent French history. And this appears to be a disagreement of considerable significance. Whereas Tocqueville laments the destruction of the aristocracy,[38] and implies throughout his work that by laying it low the revolution had thereby destroyed the mainstay of "liberty," Moore concludes quite the opposite.

> The consequence was the destruction of one of the indispensable social bases of right-wing authoritarian régimes that show a strong tendency to culminate in fascism under the impact of advanced industry. . . . Where the impulse behind the bourgeois revolution has been weak or abortive, the consequences have been in other major countries either fascism or communism. By destroying one of the major causes of such an outcome, *the survival of a landed aristocracy into modern times, and doing so in the late eighteenth century, the French Revolution made a major contribution to the development of parliamentary democracy in France.*[39]

Moore therefore differs fundamentally with Tocqueville on this issue. For while Moore sees the key elements of a liberal society — including certain basic freedoms — emerging as a result of the destruction of the French aristocracy, Tocqueville's emphasis, more often than not, is on the ascendancy of the masses and their passion for equality at the expense of liberty. In the post-revolutionary order liberty had become altogether precarious and a major reason for this was the destruction of the aristocracy as a social and political force. Whether Tocqueville was

---

[36] *Ibid.*

[37] *Ibid.*, p. 106.

[38] Tocqueville, *L'Ancien Régime et la Révolution*, p. 170.

[39] *Moore, op. cit.*, pp. 106–107 (italics added).

right or wrong about the significance he assigned to the destruction of the aristocracy, one obviously cannot even begin to settle here. But the issue is certainly important and deserves further research.

For Tocqueville the French Revolution was the first stage of the permanent democratic revolution in which the "people" had won their first victory. Indeed, Tocqueville persisted in seeing all about him and until the end of his days not merely the menace but even the victory of the forces of equality.

In the course of his intellectual career, Tocqueville had moved successively from the analytical concept "majority" to "mass" and, finally, to "class." He demonstrated brilliantly in his final great work the utility of "class" for an understanding of the old order and the sources of revolution. However, he never analyzed with the same degree of objectivity the class structure of the society of his own time and consequently never fully grasped some of its most important aspects.

For in the end, both the concentration of political power and the growth of the working class in and around Paris constituted for Tocqueville the greatest threats to what he called liberty. In fact, he saw some connection between the two phenomena that prompted him to regard the Second Empire as "socialistic." [40]

However, France under the Second Empire was anything but socialistic. For it was precisely under the régime of Napoleon III that modern, large-scale industrial capitalism enjoyed an exceptionally rapid expansion and, eventually, consolidated itself. "In the twenty years from 1850 to 1870, the value of annual industrial production doubled, and the number of establishments employing steam-driven machinery almost quadrupled." [41] Certain developments in the French economy during that period increasingly concentrated industrial production in a few hands. Under the Second Empire railway construction flourished and soon covered France. Both the construction and management of the railroads were entrusted to a few very large firms while many small ones disappeared. The railways also stimulated industrial production generally, but especially those industries directly or indirectly producing bridges, locomotives, and rails. The construction of the railways and the expansion of

---

[40] Cf. Seymour Drescher, *Dilemmas of Democracy* (Pittsburgh: University of Pittsburgh Press, 1968), p. 223.

[41] Georges Duveau, *La Vie Ouvrière en France sous le Second Empire,* (Paris: Gallimard, 1946), p. 9. These and other facts about industrial development and working-class life under Napoleon III are taken from Duveau's comprehensive study.

industry brought together large numbers of laborers, who now worked under those trying conditions with which every student of industrial development is familiar.

Workers definitely did not thrive under the régime Tocqueville called "socialistic." Under the Second Empire poverty among workers was widespread and severely felt. Real wages rose only in three or four departments, and workers had difficulty meeting their subsistence needs even in "normal" times, that is, when crisis conditions were absent and production was steadily increasing. In areas as different from each other as Alsace and Marseille, and in the comparatively good years when the price of subsistence was exceptionally low, workers remained hard-pressed; they earned their bare subsistence only with difficulty, and frequently earned less than enough to subsist on.

In the face of this reality, Tocqueville nevertheless continued to deplore the "passion for equality," never recognizing that far from equality, a new form of servitude and inequality was now winning out. A new socio-economic system, characterized by the increasing concentration of economic power, was being consolidated — a system in which large masses of people would be effectively separated from the means of controlling their fate, and would enjoy precious little of either liberty or equality.

APPENDIX.

Main Events in the Career
of Alexis Charles Henri Clerel
de Tocqueville (1805-1859)

Traveled in Italy and Sicily and recorded his impressions (1826).

Magistrate under Charles X (1827).

Studied English history and economics and attended lectures of François Guizot (1828–1830).

Journied to America with Gustave de Beaumont (May 1831–February 1832).

Wrote (with Beaumont) *Du système pénitentiaire aux États-Unis* (1833).

Wrote *De la démocratie en Amérique* (1835, 1840).

Journied to England and Ireland (1833 and again in 1835).

Wrote "Political and Social Condition of France" (1836).

Wrote *"Mémoire sur l'influence du point de départ sur l'avenir de la société des États-Unis"* (1837).

Member of the *Académie des sciences morales et politiques* (1837).

Elected to Chamber of Deputies for Valognes (1839).

Journied to Algeria as a member of a parliamentary subcommittee (1841).

Member of the National Assembly for la Manche (1848–1851).

Member of the Constitutional Commission (1848).

Foreign Minister (June–October 1849).

Arrested in the *Coup d'état* of December 2, 1851, and retired from politics.

Wrote *L'Ancien régime et la révolution* (1856).

Bibliography

Aron, Raymond. "La définition libérale de la liberté, Alexis de Tocqueville et Karl Marx," *European Journal of Sociology (Archives de Sociologie Européenne)* (1964), 5: 159–89.

————. *Main Currents in Sociological Thought.* 2 vols. London: Weidenfeld and Nicolson, 1968.

Beaumont, Gustave de, and Alexis de Tocqueville. *On the Penitentiary System in the United States and its Application in France.* Carbondale and Edwardsville: Southern Illinois University Press, 1964.

Blake, Nelson Manfred. *A History of American Life and Thought.* New York: McGraw-Hill, 1963.

Bloch, Marc. *Feudal Society.* Translated by L. A. Manyon; foreword by M. M. Postan. 2 vols. Chicago: The University of Chicago Press, 1968.

————. *Les Caractères originaux de l'histoire rurale française.* Oslo: 1931.

Bode, Carl, ed. *American Life in the 1840's.* Garden City, N.Y.: Doubleday Anchor, 1967.

Bottomore, T. B. *Classes in Modern Society.* New York: Pantheon, 1966.

————. *Elites and Society.* Baltimore: Penguin, 1967.

Bryce, James. *The Predictions of Hamilton and Tocqueville.* Johns Hopkins University Studies in Historical and Political Science, vol. 5. Edited by Herbert B. Adams. Baltimore: Johns Hopkins, 1887.

Bury, J. B. *The Idea of Progress.* New York: Dover, 1955.

The Cambridge Modern History. Vol. 11. Cambridge: At the University Press, 1909.

Chevalier, Michel. *Lettres sur l'Amérique du Nord.* Paris: 1836; translated under the title: *Society, Manners, and Politics in the United States; Being a Series of Letters on North America.* Edited by John W. Ward. Garden City, N.Y.: Doubleday Anchor, 1961.

Cobban, Alfred. *The Social Interpretation of the French Revolution*. Cambridge: At the University Press, 1968.

Davis, David Brion, ed. *Ante-Bellum Reform*. New York: Harper and Row, 1967.

Davis, James P. "Toward a Theory of Revolution," *American Sociological Review* 27 (February 1962): 5–19.

Drescher, Seymour. *Tocqueville and England*, Cambridge, Mass.: Harvard University Press, 1964.

————. *Dilemmas of Democracy: Tocqueville and Modernization*. Pittsburgh: University of Pittsburgh Press, 1968.

Duveau, Georges. *La Vie ouvrière en France sous le Second Empire*. Paris: Gallimard, 1946.

————. *1848: The Making of a Revolution*. Translated by Anne Carter. New York: Vintage, 1968.

d'Eichthal, Eugène. *Alexis de Tocqueville et la démocratie liberale*. Paris, 1897.

Gargan, Edward T. *Alexis de Tocqueville: The Critical Years 1848–1851*, Washington, D.C.: The Catholic University of America Press, 1955.

Gay, Peter. *Voltaire's Politics: The Poet as Realist*. Princeton, N.J.: Princeton University Press, 1959.

Herr, Richard. *Tocqueville and the Old Regime*. Princeton, N.J.: Princeton University Press, 1962.

Hobsbawm, Eric J. *The Age of Revolution 1789–1848*. New York: Mentor, 1962.

————. *Industry and Empire: The Making of Modern English Society*. Vol. 2. New York: Pantheon, 1968.

————, and Rudé, George. *Captain Swing*. New York: Pantheon, 1968.

Kraditor, Aileen S. *Means and Ends in American Abolitionism*. New York: Pantheon, 1967.

Labrousse, C. E. *La Crise de l'économie française à la fin de l'ancien régime et au début de la Révolution*. Vol. 1. Paris, 1944.

Laski H. J. "Alexis de Tocqueville and Democracy." In *The Social and Political Ideas of Some Representative Thinkers of the Victorian Age*, edited by F. J. C. Hearnshaw. London: Harrap, 1935.

Lefebvre, George. *The Coming of the French Revolution*. Translated by R. R. Palmer. Princeton, N. J.: Princeton University Press, 1967.

Lichtheim, George. *The Origins of Socialism*. New York and Washington: Praeger, 1969.

Lipset, Seymour Martin. *Political Man*. Garden City, N.Y.: Doubleday, 1960.

————. "Political Sociology." In *Sociology Today*, edited by Merton, Broom, and Cottrell. New York: Basic Books, 1961, pp. 84–114.

Lively, Jack. *The Social and Political Thought of Alexis de Tocqueville*. Oxford: Clarendon Press, 1962.

Martindale, Don. *Institutions, Organizations and Mass Society.* Boston: Houghton-Mifflin, 1966, p. 222.

Marx, Karl, and Engels, Frederick. *Selected Works.* 2 vols. Moscow: Foreign Languages Publishing House, 1950.

Mayer, J. P. *Alexis de Tocqueville: A Biographical Essay in Political Science.* New York: Viking, 1940.

Mills, C. Wright. *The Power Elite.* New York: Oxford, 1959.

Moore, Barrington, Jr. *Social Origins of Dictatorship and Democracy.* Boston: Beacon Press, 1968.

Mornet, Daniel. *La pensée française au XVIIIe siècle.* Paris, 1926.

——. *Les Origines Intellectuelles de la Révolution française.* Paris, 1933.

——. *Rousseau, l'Homme et l'Oeuvre.* Paris: 1950.

Nisbet, Robert A. *Emile Durkheim.* Englewood Cliffs, N.J.: Prentice-Hall, 1965.

——. *The Sociological Tradition.* New York: Basic Books, 1966.

Olsen, Marvin E. *The Process of Social Organization.* New York: Holt, Rinehart and Winston, 1968.

Pessen, Edward. *Jacksonian America: Society, Personality, and Politics.* Homewood, Ill.: Dorsey, 1969.

Pierson, George Wilson. *Tocqueville and Beaumont in America.* New York: Oxford, 1938.

Pole, J. R., ed. *The Advance of Democracy.* New York: Harper and Row, 1967.

Probst, George E., ed. *The Happy Republic.* New York: Harper Torchbooks, 1962.

"Resolutions on the Social, Civil, and Intellectual Condition of the Laboring Classes," *The Man* (New York), August 30, 1834, II, p. 357.

Richter, Melvin. "Tocqueville's Contributions to the Theory of Revolution." In *Revolution,* Nomos VIII. Edited by Carl J. Friedrich. New York: Atherton, 1966, pp. 75–121.

Rozwenc, Edwin C., ed. *Ideology and Power in the Age of Jackson.* Documents in American Civilization Series. Garden City, N.Y.: Donbleday Anchor, 1964.

de Ruggiero, G. *Storia del liberalismo europeo* (Bari, 1925). Translated by R. G. Collingwood. London, 1927.

——. "Tocqueville. . . ." *Encyclopaedia of the Social Sciences.* New York: Macmillan, 1959, vols. 13–14, pp. 646, 647.

Schlesinger, Arthur M., Jr. *The Age of Jackson.* Boston: Little, Brown, 1946.

Sée, Henri. *Évolution Commerciale et Industrielle de la France sous l'Ancien Régime.* Paris, 1925.

——. *Histoire Économique de la France.* Paris: 1939.

Soltau, R. *French Political Thought in the Nineteenth Century.* London: 1931.

Jared Sparks and Alexis de Tocqueville. Johns Hopkins University Studies in

Historical and Political Science, vol. 16, no. 12. Edited by Herbert B. Adams, Baltimore: Johns Hopkins, 1898, pp. 7–49.

Taylor, George Rogers. *The Transportation Revolution.* New York: Harper Torchbooks, 1968.

Tocqueville, Alexis de. *On the State of Society in France before the Revolution of 1789; and on the Causes Which Led to That Event.* Translated by Henry Reeve. London: John Murray, 1856.

——. *Oeuvres Complètes.* Edited by Gustave de Beaumont. 9 vols. Paris: Michel Lévy, 1860–1866.

——. *Oeuvres et Correspondance Inédites,* publiées et précédées d'une notice par Gustave de Beaumont. Paris: Michel Lévy Frères, 1861.

——. *Democracy in America.* The Henry Reeve text, revised by Frances Bowen, and further corrected and edited with an introduction, editorial, notes, and bibliographies by Phillip Bradley. New York: Knopf, 1948, 1960.

——. *Recollections.* Translated by Alexander Teixeira de Mattos; edited by J. P. Mayer. London: The Harvill Press, 1948.

——. *Oeuvres Complètes.* Édition définitive publiée sous la direction de J.P. Mayer. Paris: Gallimard, 1951–.

——. *Journeys to England and Ireland.* Translated by George Lawrence and J. P. Mayer; edited by J. P. Mayer. New Haven: Yale University Press, 1958.

——. *Journey to America.* Translated by George Lawrence; edited by J. P. Mayer. New Haven: Yale University Press, 1960.

Alexis de Tocqueville: Livre de Centenaire, 1859–1959. Editions du Centre National de la Recherche Scientifique. Paris, 1960.

Tocqueville, Alexis de, and Senior, Nassau William. *Correspondence and Conversations from 1834 to 1859.* Edited by M. C. M. Simpson. 2 vols. London: Henry S. King, 1872.

Tucker, George. *Progress of the United States in Population and Wealth in Fifty Years as Exhibited by the Decennial Census from 1790 to 1840.* Abridged. New York, 1855.

Wish, Harvey. *Society and Thought in Early America.* New York: McKay, 1950.

Index